The Art of Drama,

OTHELLO

Published by Peripeteia Press Ltd.

First published February 2023

ISBN: 978-1-913577-87-2

Check out our A-level English Literature website, peripeteia.webs.com

PERIPETEIA PRESS

—

Contents

Introduction to *The Art of Drama* series

The philosopher Nietzsche described his work as 'the greatest gift that [mankind] has ever been given' while the Elizabethan poet Edmund Spenser hoped his book *The Faerie Queene* [1590] would magically transform readers into noblemen. Two hundred years later Wordsworth and Coleridge hoped their *Lyrical Ballads* [1798] would radically improve English sensibilities. In comparison, our aims for *The Art of Drama* series of books are a little more modest. Fundamentally, we aim to provide books that will be of maximum interest and usefulness to students of English and to their teachers.

In this new series of books, we aim to reproduce the success of our *The Art of Poetry* series by providing fine-grained, well-informed, lively and engaging material on the key issues in key drama set texts. In the first book in the series, we focused on J. B. Priestley's popular old stager, *An Inspector Calls*. In the second, we turned our critical attention to Shakespeare's notoriously dark and troubling Scottish play, *Macbeth*, and in this edition, we explore one of the bard's most contentious plays, *Othello*.

As with all our poetry books, we hope this new series will appeal to English teachers as well as students of Literature. There is a plethora of material already available on *Othello* on the market. However, many books aimed at GCSE pupils present information in condensed, broken up or broken down, note and bullet pointed formats. A distinguishing feature of our critical guides is that they are, fundamentally, comprised of a series of short essays. Examination boards require GCSE students to write essays, yet rarely are they encouraged to read literary essays, not least because there's a paucity of this sort of material pitched at this age group. Although there is academic material on *Othello*, little of this is written specifically for GCSE or A-level students. Hence we have tried to fill this significant gap with essays modelling how to engage critically with Literary texts.

With the ever-increasing demands and importance of terminal exams, there's a great pressure on students and teachers to reach top grades. One way to attempt to do this is to drill students with exam technique and fill their heads with information in the hope that they will be able to regurgitate it accurately. In our opinion, that sort of production-line approach to learning cuts out an absolutely essential part of the experience of reading and writing about literature, perhaps the most rewarding and richest part, i.e., the forming of our own critical views. Good critical writing about poems, novels and plays does not merely regurgitate somebody else's ideas uncritically, rather it expresses the critical opinions of the writer, informed, of course, by their experiences in the classroom and elsewhere. No two essays on any Literary text should be exactly the same. Ideally English teaching should nurture pupils' ability to express their own critical thinking about texts in their own emerging critical voices, informed by discussion with peers and the expertise of teachers.

Our essays in this collection do not follow any specific framework or aim to hit specific assessment objectives. We are not trying to get in 12.5% of context or to make sure we always finish with a telling quote. Rather the writers of this guide have been given free rein to write about what they find most interesting about their chosen topics, whether this be a central theme, character or scene. It is our conviction that when we write about the things that most interest us we write our best work.

This new *Othello* guide is aimed primarily at GCSE students aiming for the top grades and at A-level English Literature students, as well as teachers and lecturers. Some sections of the guide will be valuable to pupils at both key stages, but others, such as the material on the critical reception of the play over time will be most useful to A-level students. Our material seeks to stimulate a critical response, which might include fervent agreement or strong disagreement. We aim to make students think critically, to reflect, compare and evaluate different critical views as part of the process of formulating their own.

Writing about plays

The play and the novel

Plays and novels have several significant features in common, such as characters, dialogue, plots and settings. In addition, students read plays in lessons, often sitting at desks in the same way as they read novels. So it's not surprising that many students treat these two related, but distinct, literary art forms as if they were indistinguishable. Time and again, teachers and examiners come across sentences such as 'In the novel *Othello*...' Though sometimes this can be just a slip of the pen, often this error is a good indicator of a weak grasp of the nature of the text. Stronger responses fully appreciate the fact that *Othello* is a play, written for the stage by a playwright and realise the implications of the writer's choice of the dramatic form. We can track some of these implications by considering the different opportunities for characterisation and settings provided by the page and the stage.

Characterisation

Imagine you're a novelist writing a scene introducing a major character. Survey the rich variety of means at your disposal: You could begin with a quick pen portrait of their appearance using your narrative voice, or you could have your characters say or do something significant. Alternatively, you could utilise your narrator to provide comments about, and background on, the character. Then again, you might take us into the character's thoughts and reveal what's really going on inside their head. If you're trying to convey thought as it happens you could even use a stream of consciousness.

Now imagine that you're a playwright introducing a major character. Consider the far more limited means at your disposal. Though you could describe a character's appearance, you'd have to communicate this through stage directions, which, of course, a theatre audience would not be able to read or hear. The same holds true for background information and narratorial style comments about the character, none of which would an audience be able to read. And unless you are going to use the dramatic devices known as the

---

7

aside and the soliloquy, as Shakespeare famously used in his great tragedies, you will struggle to find a direct way to show what your character's thinking. As a playwright, stage action and dialogue, however, are your meat and drink. While for a novelist being able to write cracking dialogue is a useful part of the repertoire, for a dramatist it's essential.

In general, drama focuses our attention on the outward behaviour of characters. Skilfully done, this can, of course, also reveal their interior thoughts. Nevertheless, novels more easily give access to the workings of the mind. You may have noticed this when novels are adapted into films and directors have to make the decision about whether to use a voiceover to convey the narrator or characters' thoughts. Rarely does this work well.

Settings

With a swish of his or her fountain pen or deft fingers running over a keyboard, a novelist can move quickly and painlessly from one setting to another. One chapter of a novel could be set in a medieval village, the next on a far distant planet in the far distant future. The only limitation is the novelist's skill in rendering these worlds. What is true for geographical settings is also true for temporal ones. A novelist can write 'One thousand years later...' or track a character from cradle to grave. A novelist can also play around with narrative time, using flashbacks and flashforwards.

Though a little more restricted, a modern film director can also move fairly easily between geographical and temporal settings and can cross-cut between them. But not so a playwright. Why? Because plays are written for an actual physical stage and radically changing a stage set during the action of a play is a tricky, potentially cumbersome business. Imagine a medieval village, with its ramshackle thatched huts, pig pens and dirty streets. How are you going to transform this stage set to the dizzyingly futuristic world of Planet Zog in 2188 A.D. without the audience really noticing?

Possibly stage technicians could dismantle and construct the different stage sets while the audience waits patiently for the action to restart. But wouldn't that be clumsy and rather break the spell you'd hope your play was weaving?

More likely you'd use a break, perhaps between the scenes or, better, during the interval for the major re-arrangement of stage scenery. Practically speaking, how many different stage sets could you create for a single play? Minimalistic stage designs might allow you to employ more settings, but you'd still be far more restricted than a film director or a novelist. And then there's the expense of building elaborate sets. Theatres aren't usually flush with money, but complex stage sets are likely to be expensive. Another way out of this problem would be to have a pretty much bare and unchanging stage set and convey changes in scenes through the dialogue, a technique Shakespeare had to use for The Globe stage. Think, for instance, of the start of *The Tempest*, where the action of the opening scene takes place on a boat out a sea.

Here's our version of this sort of minimalist, setting-through-dialogue technique:

Stage direction: Two characters meet on a bare stage.
Character 1: What is this strange, futuristic place with extraordinary buildings?
Character 2: Why, this is the capital city of the Planet Zog.
Character 1: Aha! And, unless I'm mistaken, the year is now 2188 A.D.

etc.
As we'll see, Shakespeare tends to do this with a little more subtlety.

The action in plays also tends to take place in chronological order, with time moving forward in a linear direction. Partly this is because as we watch plays in real time, it's difficult to convey to an audience that a particular scene is actually a flashback. There are exceptions, of course, to the chronological trend. Notably Harold Pinter's *Betrayal*, for instance, in which the action of the play unfolds backwards from the present to past.

The time frame of a play also tends to be limited – days, weeks, perhaps even months, but very rarely years, decades or centuries. After all, it's not easy for an actor, or series of actors, to convincingly present characters ageing over a prolonged period.

Venice and Cyprus

Two questions shape this section on the play's two major settings: Why did Shakespeare choose these two specific places and what does the shift from Venice to Cyprus in Act II signify? Superficially at least, Venice and Cyprus appear to be binary opposites. Located at the heart of Christian European civilisation, in Shakespeare's day the wealthy city state of Venice was famous for its vibrant commerce and cultural sophistication. In the first act of *Othello*, it is presented as a state governed by law and order. For example, when Brabantio's sleep is disturbed by Iago and Roderigo's rowdiness in the streets and their talk of robbery, he is shocked because such unruly behaviour is happening in Venice. Moreover, later in the same Act, the potential violent dispute between Brabantio and Othello is settled justly through a calm, semi-legal process by Lodovico and the Senate. Here, a charge is cited, witnesses are brought forth, evidence is weighed and then justice is dispensed. By defending Cyprus, Venice is also presented as a protector of the Christian world from the threat of the powerful and expansionist Ottoman Empire.

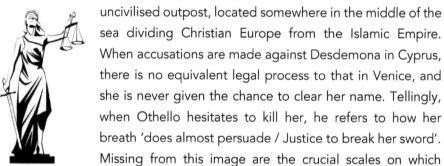

In contrast, Elizabethans thought of Cyprus as a wild, lawless island, an uncivilised outpost, located somewhere in the middle of the sea dividing Christian Europe from the Islamic Empire. When accusations are made against Desdemona in Cyprus, there is no equivalent legal process to that in Venice, and she is never given the chance to clear her name. Tellingly, when Othello hesitates to kill her, he refers to how her breath 'does almost persuade / Justice to break her sword'. Missing from this image are the crucial scales on which evidence must be weighed before a reliable verdict is reached. Although in the play Cyprus is presented as being imperilled by the threat of Turkish invasion, in fact, the island had already been conquered by the Ottomans in 1571, so it may have been thought of as part of that hostile and alien culture.

To answer our second question then, ostensibly the move from Venice to Cyprus is a move from a highly civilised society to an uncivilised, or at least far less civilised, one. Cyprus lacks an authority figure as powerful as Lodovico, or the equivalent legislative institution to the Senate. Additionally, Iago engineers the removal of its closet equivalent, Cyprus' governor Montano, so that he does not interfere with the events after his wounding in Act II. The loosening of civilised values and of the constraints of law and order in Cyprus allow Iago more licence, with less fear of exposure and punishment. Once the threat of the Turkish fleet is removed, martial discipline becomes lax, the island is given over to revelry, he is even freer to carry out his diabolic scheming.

In summary, many critics have argued that Venice embodies the secure values and norms of civilisation and that the hot, wild, freer climate of Cyprus allows these values and norm to buckle and become distorted.

However, the binary reading of Venice as civilised and Cyprus as barbaric has also been challenged by some critics. They point out that Venice's reputation was rather mixed for Shakespeare's contemporaries. In particular, Venice was infamous for its sexual tolerance and its courtesans and there appears to have been a general belief in Elizabethan culture that Venetian women were peculiarly licentious. There were also good reasons why the English might have identified with Cyprus. Like Cyprus, England is an island, of course, and at this point in history, one imperilled, like Cyprus, by the threat of powerful foreign enemies, in England's case by France, Spain and the Catholic Church. As we shall see, some critics also argue that Cyprus has features in common with the restorative 'greenworld' spaces of Shakespeare's comedies.

If we examine how the two settings are actually presented in the play, we can see that their relationship is indeed more subtle and complex than it might first appear. Shakespeare chose, for instance, to set all the scenes in Venice during the night. In some important ways, rather than being a place of light,

BARBARIE — CIVILISATION

Venice is, in fact, a place of darkness. Think, for instance, of the virulent racism and the sexism freely expressed in Act I. In contrast, the liberty Cyprus affords could, potentially, have made it a demi-paradise, a place of love, if it had not been for the snake in the grass, Iago. In his recent book, *Shakespearean Tragedy*, Kiernan Ryan pulls this line of thinking together when he argues that Iago is not a 'monstrous deviation from the civilised Venetian norm, but the unmasked incarnation of its actual barbarity', not Venice's 'demonic antithesis but its grotesque epitome'. The moral darkness the play uncovers is not native to Cyprus, or for that matter found in Moorishness, but is embodied, rather, in Iago who, according to Ryan, is 'terrifyingly typical of his and our world'.

In some readings of the play, Iago is even an agent of Venetian society, doing the state's dirty business by identifying threatening others and punishing their transgressions. As with all the major binaries in the play, then, the settings present a complex relationship between things that initially appear to be simple opposites.

The stage and the page

Few writers excel in both the novel and the play as literary forms [Samuel Beckett, Anton Chekhov and Michael Frayn come to mind] which underlines the point about the different demands of writing for the stage and for the page. Novels take place in the reader's mind or ear; plays take place in an actual physical space on an actual stage. For the latter to happen a whole load of people other than the writer have to be involved – directors, actors, designers, producers, technicians and so forth. This takes us to the heart of another crucial difference between reading a play, reading a novel and seeing a play on a stage. When we're reading a novel, the novelist can fill in the details of what is happening around the dialogue, such as gestures made by the characters:

'Did they even have pig-pens in medieval villages?' asked Mikey, cocking his left eyebrow in a typically quizzical manner.

When we **read** a play, sometimes these details are apparent from stage directions. However, on the page we cannot see what characters are doing while other characters are speaking. So it's easy for us to forget that silent characters are present in a scene and that their presence may significantly affect the action. When we **watch** a play, however, the actors on stage reveal how their characters are reacting to the scene and these reactions often convey crucial information about relationships, feelings and atmosphere. What, for example, is Othello doing while Brabantio is traducing him to the Senate? There are no stage directions in the play for how Othello listens. Instead, actors and directors have to decide whether Othello stares at Brabantio or perhaps looks steadily at Lodovico or perhaps avoids eye contact with anyone at all. Indeed, being alert to different staging opportunities is one of the imaginative pleasures of reading a play. Reading this way, we become directors of our own productions of *Othello*.

Without the visual dimension of the stage, it is easy for readers to ignore the things that are supposed to be happening in the narrative background while each character is speaking. If a play on a page is similar to a musical score awaiting performance, a play on the stage is the full concert.

Appreciation of the differences between a novel and a play, helps students to notice the key skills of the playwright. And focusing on the dramatic devices used by a playwright has a double benefit: firstly, all good analytical literary essays concentrate on the writer's craft; secondly, such a focus emphasises to the examiner that students understand the nature of the type of text they are exploring, viz. a play, and distinguishes them from other readers who don't really appreciate this fact. In the next section we'll focus our attention on the playwright's writing skills by focusing on stagecraft.

Stagecraft

When you're writing about a novel, it's always productive to focus on narration. Narration includes narrative perspective, such as first and third person, types of narrator, such as naïve and unreliable, as well as narrative techniques, such as the use of dialogue, cross-cuts and flashbacks. Narration is worth focusing your attention on because it's an absolutely integral feature of all novels and short stories. In plays, the equivalent of narration is stagecraft. Examining stagecraft is an incisive and revealing way to explore the writer at work.

Some playwrights are able to use all the craft and resources of the theatre – lighting, costumes, management of entrances and exits, stage set, props and music - while for various reasons [technical, artistic, budgetary] other playwrights may be more restricted. Shakespeare, for instance, doesn't really use lighting in his plays, except notably in *The Winter's Tale* [1611], because most of his plays were performed at the Globe theatre and in broad daylight. However, as we will go on to explore, often Shakespeare set scenes at night, in darkness, the first Act of *Othello* being a prime example. Of course, all theatre is an illusion, a pretence willingly shared by the audience. The stage is not the real world and the people on it are not who they say they are; they are actors, playing parts. They are also not speaking verbatim, but in carefully worked verse. But we accept them as real for the duration of the play. For the Globe audience, the disjuncture between what they could see on stage and what they could hear in Shakespeare's words was even more acute. By engaging the audience's imaginations through the power of his words Shakespeare could make them feel darkness and night-time, even if they couldn't actually see it.

Lighting

Lighting can be used starkly and boldly, such as in picking out a main character in a bright spotlight, or it can be used more subtly to convey mood and generate atmosphere. Intense white light makes everything look stark. Blue lights help create a sense of coolness, whereas yellows, oranges and reds generate a sense of warmth and even passion. Floor lights can light an actor from beneath, making them look powerful and threatening. Light coming down on them from above can cause an actor to look vulnerable and threatened or even angelic. Changes of lighting between scenes are common ways of changing the pervasive atmosphere.

However, for most of his theatrical career, Shakespeare was writing for the Globe theatre where performances took place only during daylight hours. Only when his plays were performed at the indoor theatre at Blackfriars, from around 1608, could Shakespeare employ lighting effects. This, however, doesn't mean that Shakespeare doesn't create lighting effects, rather that he does so through the language rather than through stage directions.

Obviously, as have noted already, *Othello* starts at night and the action remains in darkness until the characters arrive in Cyprus at the start of Act II. The fact that for the original Globe audience experienced all this in daylight emphasises the symbolic dimensions of this darkness: an epicentre of civilisation is associated not with light, but with a darkness that could be interpreted as a moral benightedness. In addition, the fact that the audience can see what the characters cannot suggests a perceptual darkness or ignorance.

Costumes

Shakespeare's instructions on costume are also limited, usually embedded within the texts, rather than stated separately in stage directions. Think, for example, of Malvolio's yellow cross-gartered stockings or Hamlet's inky suit of woe. On the other hand, the importance of costumes is underlined repeatedly in Shakespeare's plays by characters who disguise themselves by changing their clothes. For instance, Viola becoming Cesario in *Twelfth Night* [1602] Kent and Edmund disguising themselves in *King Lear* [1606]. Repeatedly, villainy in Shakespeare's plays tries to remain hidden under a layer of polished manners and fine clothes. Lady Macbeth's famous injunction to her husband in *Macbeth* [1606] is to look 'like the innocent flower / But be the serpent under't'. Iago, of course, disguises his villainy underneath a façade of friendship and loyalty. A production might choose to dress him in the plain clothes of an ordinary soldier to conceal his extraordinary nature and to distinguish him from more lavishly dressed characters, such as Othello and Cassio.

The general sparsity of information about costumes has, however, allowed directors over the years to relocate Shakespeare's plays to all sorts of settings with a huge variety of matching costumes. In a recent RSC production of *Antony and Cleopatra* [1607], for instance, the designs for the Egyptian queen's costumes were inspired by powerful contemporary female celebrities such as Beyoncé.

Entrances and exits

When a playwright is restricted in the range of stagecraft he or she can utilise, not only do the devices they employ become more prominent, but other integral aspects of stage business also become more significant. In *Othello* the timing of exits and entrances are particularly important. Consider, for instance, the moments when Iago conveniently removes himself from a scene or when Roderigo arrives in one. If the timing was only slightly different, Iago's plotting with Roderigo would be discovered. Or consider the entrance of

Brabantio and his followers in the first Act when they seek to arrest Othello. Such an entrance generates tension on stage and provides opportunities for different ways of staging it.

Stage sets

As we mentioned in our discussion of the key differences between novels and plays, the latter invariably have fewer settings due to the fact that dramatic texts have to be physically realised in stage designs. And, as we also noted, changing from one elaborate stage set to another presents problems for directors and, potentially for the finances of a production. What sort of choices does a stage designer have to make when creating a set? Firstly, a lot depends on the nature of the play, as well as the playwright, the director and the budget. Some playwrights are very particular about the settings of their plays and describe them in tremendous detail.

The American playwright Tennessee Williams, for instance, wrote particularly lyrical stage directions, such as those that open his play *A Streetcar Named Desire*: 'First dark of an evening in May' and the 'sky is a peculiarly tender blue, almost turquoise, which invests the scene with a kind of lyricism and gracefully attenuates the atmosphere of decay'. If that isn't enough to get a stage designer to shake and scratch their head, Williams finishes with a synesthetic poetic flourish - 'you can almost feel the warm breath of the brown river'. Imagine being asked to create that effect on stage.

Other playwrights will sketch out far more minimalistic sets. Samuel Beckett in *Waiting for Godot*, for instance, describes the stage set in the sparest way possible, using just six simple words: 'A country road. A tree. Evening'. Even if the playwright doesn't provide a great deal of information about the exact setting, a director is likely to have an overall concept for a play and insist, albeit to varying degrees, that the set design fits with this. If, for instance, a director wishes to bring out the contemporary political resonances of a play such as *Julius Caesar* she or he might dress the characters like well-known American politicians and set the play in a place looking a little like the modern White House. Similarly, Shakespeare's *Richard III* has often been relocated to an imagined modern fascistic state.

Given free rein, a stage designer has to decide how realistic, fantastical, symbolic and/or expressionist their stage set will be. The attempt to represent what looks like the real world on stage, as if the audience are looking in through an invisible fourth wall, is called verisimilitude and is the equivalent of photographic realism in fine art.

Stage sets for *Othello*

What are the various spaces that directors and stage designers have to create for a production of *Othello*? Obviously, there are the two major locations of Venice and Cyprus. How might you arrange the Globe stage to indicate these very different places? Perhaps some flags and a few well-chosen items of furniture? In addition, there are various public spaces in Venice, the Senate meeting room, a harbour in Cyprus, the place where Othello overhears Cassio's conversation with Bianca and, of course, Desdemona's bedroom.

All of these spaces are much more easily created in realistic ways on film or

even on a modern stage compared with the much more limited space and resources of the Globe theatre. In the 1995 film of *Othello*, directed by Oliver Parker, for instance, some of the scenes in which Iago infects Othello's mind take place in an armoury, while the Cassio-Bianca exchange happens in a dungeon where prisoners appear to have been tortured. Consider, in contrast how, if you were directing the play for the Globe theatre how you might get Desdemona's bed onto the stage. A potentially large item would be hard to wheel on without distracting the audience's attention. As with lighting, the lack of verisimilitude on the Globe stage means that these spaces have to be generated in the audience's imaginations, mostly through the evocative power of Shakespeare's words.

Props

Props can also be used as emblems of character - heroes in Shakespeare's plays invariably brandish and use swords, while Machiavellian villains, such as

Iago, Claudius and Goneril use poison. Unlike the other two, in Iago's case, of course, he doesn't need to carry an actual bottle of poison secreted on his person but uses poisonous language to infect Othello's mind. In *Macbeth* villains or characters carrying out villainous acts, such as Macbeth's murder of King Duncan, carry daggers, not swords. Aware of this, perhaps an enterprising production could arm Iago with a dagger, rather than a sword, and also have Othello kill himself with a dagger.

Other than the ubiquitous swords, what other props feature prominently in *Othello*? There are several letters concerning the official business of the Senate, various torches and lights, including the lights in Desdemona's bedroom, wine bottles in the scene where Cassio is intoxicated and most famously, even notoriously, the handkerchief given to Desdemona by Othello.

In many of Shakespeare's plays physical letters are forged or intercepted or fall dangerously into the wrong hands, moving the plot forward. Such letters are important because they seem to provide hard, physical, almost always undeniable evidence of wrongdoing; it's hard to deny what's there in black and white. In *Hamlet* several crucial letters are sent, intercepted or received by their attended addressee; in *King Lear* the villain Edmund forges a letter from his brother Edgar expressing hostility to their father; in *Twelfth Night* Malvolio is undone by a forged letter. It is telling that Iago has no need to forge a letter in order to convince Othello of Desdemona's betrayal. Iago could, perhaps, have forged an impassioned love letter from Cassio to Desdemona or from her to him and this, surely, would have been stronger evidence than the words Iago claims to have heard Cassio speak while asleep. As we shall argue with the handkerchief, the lack of proper, convincing evidence emphasises how readily Othello accepts Iago's insinuations.

As we've noted, torches and lights are used to indicate the action is taking place in a darkness that, on the Globe stage at least, would have been more obviously metaphorical than literal. Wine bottles and a proliferation of drinking vessels could be used to indicate the change in Cyprus from a disciplined war-footing to a place of pleasure and revelry.

Whereas critics have not paid these props any great deal of attention, the same cannot be said for the handkerchief given by Othello to Desdemona and lost by her to Iago.

The Handkerchief

Commenting on the play in 1693, the writer Thomas Rymer was famously scathing about the dramatic function of the handkerchief. Rymer claimed that Othello ought to be renamed 'The Tragedy of the Handkerchief' and that the play's moral was a warning that women should better look after their linen. Rymer, like other subsequent critics, felt that it was absurd for so much weight to be put in the play on such a ridiculously insubstantial object. In *Shakespearean Tragedy*, Kiernan Ryan neatly turns Rymer's reasoning on its head. Arguing that Shakespeare's use of this prop is not a weakness, but a dramatic strength, Ryan writes that the handkerchief's 'very triviality as a flimsy piece of cloth' is what makes it a perfect symbol for the fragility of a marriage 'blighted by male fears of female sexuality'. We would add to this the fact that such paltry evidence is enough to persuade Othello of his wife's betrayal indicates how predisposed he is to trust Iago and to distrust his wife and all women.

Many critics have noted how the handkerchief passes through a number of different hands during the play, linking, for instance, all the female characters together. The virginal innocent, Desdemona, the world-wise wife, Emilia, and the supposed courtesan, Bianca, all handle this object. This has led some critics to speculate about the different connections the female characters have with the handkerchief. Some, for example, have speculated as to why Bianca is unable to make a copy of this object. One explanation is that the handkerchief symbolises a valid marriage and that, as a supposed prostitute, Bianca cannot replicate this. Other critics have argued that the handkerchief does, indeed, symbolise Othello and Desdemona's marriage, but point to the way this would suggest the marriage is based on faith, belief and magic rather than mutual love and trust. In addition, it is clear from the play that Othello and Desdemona view the handkerchief very differently. Whereas for Othello it is a magical, almost sacred, intrinsically African object, for Desdemona it is just an attractive piece of cloth.

Another common interpretive move is to read the handkerchief as symbolising Desdemona herself. Both are treated as white objects, owned, displayed and argued over. Moreover, while the handkerchief's whiteness reflects her innocence, the design of the red strawberries is often interpreted as symbolising the blood she will 'lose' on her wedding night. These critics often make a link too between the handkerchief and Desdemona's bedsheets. The strawberry design has also been interpreted as symbolic, with some critics opining it is 'double-coded' as strawberries are both beautiful and can contain worms.

Sound effects & music

There are a few references to sounds off-stage in the play, specifically canon or perhaps rifle shots fired in honour of the arrival of Othello's ship in Cyprus in Act II and trumpets that herald his entrance. In the context of the potential conflict with the Ottomans, shots could have been alarming, but read in this way, they turn out to be false alarms.

Music is a highly effective device for developing mood and atmosphere. There's a curious scene at the start of Act III when Cassio and the clown enter with some musicians and Cassio bids them play 'something that's brief' in celebration. Although there are no stage directions describing this music, the clown's unimpressed and punning response indicates that the musicians play wind instruments, perhaps rather badly. Often this scene is cut from productions, but if it is included, a director will have to decide on an appropriate piece of music. Iago's reference to untuning Othello's love might suggest that the music here should be ominous in some way, either inappropriately mournful, rather than celebratory, or badly played and out of tune.

In contrast, Desdemona's willow song in Act IV, scene 3 is horribly appropriate and poignant. It is a song about one of her mother's maids, the significantly named Barbary, who was abandoned by her lover and died lamenting this loss of love. Clearly the song echoes Desdemona's fate and makes a parallel between her and Barbary. It is a melancholic song too, likely to generate feelings of sadness in the audience. Significantly, Desdemona is also not able to remember all the words, just as she isn't able to anticipate what will happen to her only a few scenes later.

The nature of the play

What is a tragedy?

The exact nature of the literary genre we call 'tragedy' is much debated. According to *The Complete A-Z English Literature Handbook* a tragedy is a 'drama which ends disastrously' and falls into two broad types:

- Greek tragedy, where fate brings about the downfall of the character[s].
- Shakespearean tragedy, where a character has free will and their fatal flaw causes the downfall.

It is hard to argue that the tragedy in *Othello* is caused by fate, as it is so clearly engineered by human agency, not least by Iago's machinations, so this definition doesn't fit the play. Although the second definition seems closer to *Othello*, as we shall discover, the second half of the definition, specifically the claim that the hero's fatal flaw causes their downfall, is much disputed by literary academics and Shakespeare scholars.

According to Jennifer Wallace in *The Cambridge Introduction to Tragedy*, 'Tragedy is an art form created to confront the most difficult experiences we face; death, loss, injustice, thwarted passion, despair'. Wallace goes on to explain that 'questions about the causes of suffering, which are raised in each culture, are posed powerfully in tragedy'.[1] That's helpful, but couldn't we say the same sorts of things about the academic subjects of philosophy and religious studies?

While, on the one hand, there are critics, such as Terry Eagleton, who argue the only thing that the plays we label as tragedies have in common is that they are 'very, very sad', on the other, many critics opine that all literary tragedies share common, distinctive formal features which separate them from real-life stories of great unhappiness. And, if we shrink our perspective down from tragedies as a whole art form to Shakespeare's versions, we'll discover there's not much academic agreement either about what attributes these types of plays share:

'An eminent Shakespearean scholar famously remarked that there is no such thing as Shakespearean Tragedy; there are only Shakespearean tragedies'.

So begins Tom McAlindon's essay *What is a Shakespearian Tragedy?*[2] The author goes on to point out how attempts to define tragedy, such as those we've quoted above, tend to 'give a static impression of the genre and incline towards prescriptivism', ignoring the fact that genres are constantly changing and developing over time.

To sum up: the definition of what makes a play a 'tragedy' is contested. So too is the definition of what constitutes a Shakespearean Tragedy. Indeed, more fundamentally, the idea of defining both these terms is itself contested within literary criticism. Where does that leave us? Perhaps a sensible way to try to find a route out of the academic fogginess is to start at the beginning and then navigate our way from that fixed point. In terms of defining tragedy as an art form, Aristotle's theories of tragedy serve well as a starting point.

---

[1] Wallace, *The Cambridge Introduction to Tragedy*.

[2] McEachern [ed.], *The Cambridge Companion to Tragedy*, p.1.

Aristotle

Often it is assumed that Aristotle was setting down a prescriptivist rulebook for writing tragedies, a kind of classical instruction manual for aspiring playwrights to follow slavishly. This assumption is mistaken. In fact, Aristotle, in his *Poetics*, was describing the features of classical tragedies as he saw them. Taken as prescriptivist or descriptivist, what is certain is that Aristotle's ideas about tragedies have been massively influential. In particular, four key ideas have helped shape the ways tragedies have been written, performed and read for hundreds of years. These ideas concern:

  i.   the nature of the protagonist
  ii.   the cause of tragic action
  iii. the significance of plot
  iv.   the emotional effect of tragedy on an audience.

For our purposes, the first two of these concepts are particularly interesting. The protagonist in classical tragedy is always high-born, a prince or king or someone of equivalent status. This means their fall is as precipitous, destructive and dramatic as possible - right from the top to the very bottom of society [imagine an elephant falling off a skyscraper] in a way that the fall of someone from the bottom to the bottom of society [imagine a mouse falling off a kerb] would not be. As the tragic hero or heroine is high-born and they fall a long way down, the impact of their fall causes immense damage to society, sending shockwaves out across the whole world of the play, creating cracks and fissures across the social landscape.

Crucially, according to Aristotle, the primary cause of the fall is a fault in the tragic protagonist. Historically Shakespearean critics often conceived of this tragic flaw, or hamartia, in character-based or psychological terms. Pre-twentieth century critics often identified Othello's jealousy as his hamartia. Read through an Aristotelian critical perspective, *Othello* is a play fundamentally about its titular hero, whose tragic fall is precipitated by his hamartia. Different critics argue about what this hamartia might be but agree that Othello is at fault.

Modern criticism

However, most modern Shakespearean critics argue that an Aristotelian approach to tragedy over-emphasises the importance of the tragic hero and of characters in general. After the cataclysmic experience of World War II, literary critics became more interested in the role of society and of the power of history and of ideology to shape the experience of characters. Read through this modern perspective, individuals appear to have less agency than earlier critics had assumed and are seen as products of particular cultures and societies. Shifting critical attention away from individuals to the societies that made them, modern critics view tragedies as stemming from irresolvable, conflicting forces at work within the period in which Shakespeare was writing, a period that historians call the early modern. So, for instance, a modern critic might argue that *Othello* stages a conflict between traditional, essential feudal values – of loyalty, duty, honour, revenge and so forth – embodied in the character of the noble Moor and a new Renaissance spirit of individualism, questioning and self-determination, as exemplified in toxic form by Iago.

Tragedy and comedy

In Shakespeare's other major tragedies, such as *Hamlet* and *King Lear*, the impact of the fall of the hero, and the collateral deaths of others, sends shockwaves through society. At the start of *Othello* it seems like this story will have similarly major geopolitical ramifications. However, when the threat of the Turkish fleet is removed by the storm, the scale and scope of the tragedy seems to shrink, narrowing down to what some critics have termed a 'domestic tragedy', a play essentially about the relationship between a man and his wife. Although Desdemona and Othello's deaths are tragically poignant, they will not change anything fundamentally in Venetian society. Whereas at the end of *Hamlet* Denmark is invaded by the Norwegian prince, Fortinbras, and in *King Lear* power is passed to a new generation, in *Othello*, Cassio is simply given Othello's place and things are expected to go on as before.

This is not to say that *Othello* is a less powerful or poignant tragedy. Several critics have noted the absence of a sub-plot in the play and how this contributes to the distinctively claustrophobic sense of entrapment and of tragic inevitability in *Othello*. The narrower frame can intensify and concentrate tension.

Several critics have also explored the comedic elements of *Othello* and how these too might actually amplify its tragic power. Act I has even been seen as like a complete comedy in microcosm. In the essay on the play in her recent book *This is Shakespeare*, Emma Smith outlines these comic aspects:

1. The theme of sexual jealousy is common in comedies
2. The play features lovers whose relationship is obstructed by their family
3. Iago can be read as a trickster figure and/or as the clever, self-seeking servant.
4. Brabantio fits the character type of the outraged father
5. Othello is a deceived older husband who thinks he has been cuckolded
6. Roderigo is a dupe exploited for his money
7. The action of the play is dictated by plotting and intrigue not by geopolitical forces or by powerful fate
8. The reliance on a handkerchief as proof of Desdemona's infidelity
9. The Cassio/Bianca scene when they are overheard by a hidden Othello is similar to many scenes in the comedies
10. Cyprus can be read as being like the regenerative 'greenworld' spaces of the comedies, a freer space to which courtly characters can retreat in order to rejuvenate. However, according to Smith, Cyprus actually becomes an 'internal furnace' in which the negative aspects of characters and their society are not resolved but instead become 'more pronounced and destructive'.

Critics suggest that the continuing presence of these comic elements, including a clown, keeps open a possibility, albeit a rather remote one, that the play might end happily, right up until Desdemona's death. Furthermore this small hope, flickering like a weak flame throughout the play, makes the actual ending all the more dark and devastating.

The playwright

Had we but the space and time [as well as the skill, the scholarship and, indeed, the inclination] we could, perhaps, provide you with an exhaustive account of the life and work of the world's most famous writer. After all, the Shakespeare scholar, James Shapiro managed to write a highly engaging account of just one year, albeit a monumentally creative year, in the bard's relatively short life.[3] On the other hand, notoriously, very little information actually exists about Shakespeare's life; famously one of the only extant official documents is his will and its curious instruction to leave his wife his second-best bed. Of course, that gaping biographical hole hasn't stopped scholars, biographers and novelists leaping in and filling it with all sorts of colourful speculations, such as the story that Shakespeare originally fled Stratford because he'd been illegally poaching deer or the preposterous idea that Shakespeare didn't really write his own plays, nor presumably all of his own poems, because he wasn't from the right class.

But, we haven't the space or time to be so fanciful. So, what can usefully be said about William Shakespeare [1564-1616] in a couple of pages or so? Firstly, that he was a middle-class boy, grammar school educated, and that he didn't attend either of the great universities of Oxford or Cambridge. This fact partly accounts for the claim that Shakespeare couldn't have written his plays

---

[3] Shapiro, *1606, The Year of Lear*.

as, so the argument goes, he had neither the life experiences nor the sophisticated education to do so, a claim unpleasantly whiffing of snobbery. How did a middle-class boy from the provinces write so brilliantly about kings, queens and princes and different times and cultures? Perhaps he read widely, observed keenly and used his prodigious intelligence and imagination.

Secondly, at the tender age, even for Elizabethans, of just eighteen Shakespeare married an older woman, Anne Hathaway, who was twenty-six and already pregnant. This is a point to be borne in mind whenever Shakespeare is writing about disinherited and bitter children, those born out of wedlock and therefore labelled as 'bastards' in his world, and about fatherhood.

Thirdly, Shakespeare was an actor. Many scholars think he probably took roles, although only relatively minor ones, in his own plays. He was a member of an acting group, called the Lord Chamberlain's Men, who had a theatre built to house their performances – the Globe theatre.

Fourthly, Shakespeare was not only a highly successful playwright, but also a shrewd businessman. By middle-age he had become wealthy enough to buy the 'second largest' house in Stratford. By this time, his acting company had been promoted up the social ladder to 'The King's Men', with a royal charter and King James I as their patron, and they had purchased a second theatre.

Fifthly, Shakespeare was a highly accomplished poet as well as a playwright. Writing a decent sonnet was considered *de rigueur* for an Elizabethan courtier. Shakespeare did not write one decent sonnet, no, of course not, he wrote a sonnet sequence, a bigger and better and more sophisticated sonnet sequence than anyone has managed before or since, arguably. Comprising over a hundred and fifty sonnets, the sequence dramatizes the story of an intense love triangle, involving Shakespeare, a handsome young man and a dark lady.

Sixthly, Shakespeare is absolutely everywhere. He is the only writer whose work has by law to be studied in English schools. His poems and plays are read, studied and performed across the globe, from Australia to China, from India to Zambia, and have been translated into almost every major language, including Klingon[4]. Unsurprisingly, he's the best-selling writer ever. Estimates suggest that there have been over four hundred film versions of his plays. Phrases and words Shakespeare coined are used every day by thousands, perhaps millions, of people, sometimes consciously and sometimes because they have become an integral part of the fabric of our language. And that's still not the be-all and end-all: His head appears on bank notes, cups and tea-towels and he is a crucial part of the English tourism industry and our national identity. In this country alone, there are several theatre companies dedicated to his work, including a royal one, the RSC. In short, Shakespeare was, and is still, a cultural phenomenon.

Some critics suggest that the boy from Stratford got lucky, that his work spread across the globe by piggybacking on trade and colonialisation. First the Elizabethans and then later the Victorians explored and conquered much of the globe and everywhere the English went they took Shakespeare along with them. But, even then, that doesn't explain why Shakespeare, rather than any other English writer, became so ubiquitous. Perhaps it has something to do with the output and quality of his writing. Scholars agree that Shakespeare wrote about thirty-seven plays, one of which, *Cardelio*, has been lost.

---

[4] Apparently 'taH pagh taHbe' is Klingon for the very famous opening to a speech by Hamlet.

Shakespeare's world

Picture this: A happy, stable, highly ordered, hierarchical society in which each man and woman knows their place and, moreover, knows that this place has been rightfully assigned and fixed for them by God. All things on earth are held together in God's great, universal chain of being. Furthermore, this fixed and eternal orderliness on earth mirrors the fixed, eternal order of the heavens. As God rules the heavens so the monarch, God's representative, rules the earth. And the present monarch, Good Queen Bess, Gloriana, is a semi-divine virgin queen who has ruled peacefully for four decades. A bucolic, Edenic society in which an especially blessed race of men live harmoniously with each other and with nature, England is a demi-paradise. Recent religious conflicts between Catholics and Protestants have been resolved. The arts are blossoming as never before. Trade with the rest of the world is flourishing. Sending her ships out across the furthest seas, England is becoming a global super-power, bringing peace and prosperity for all. It is a veritable golden age. A merrie England.

The only problem with this enchanting picture is that it is, according to modern literary critics and historians, largely just that, a picture, a construct, an attractive illusion, one that helped the second Elizabethan age [1952-2022] find a desirable image of itself in the first. Whether Queen Elizabeth I's reign was ever a golden age is a matter of historical debate, but what is not really disputed is that by around 1603, the time Shakespeare was writing *Othello*, England had become a very different country and a much more turbulent and troubled place. To borrow a term from Gothic studies, at the fag-end of Elizabeth's reign and the start of James the First's England existed in a liminal space, uneasily stuck between its medieval, feudal past and a new, early modern world still in the process of coming into being. According to Lawrence Stone, there was an 'almost hysterical demand for order at all costs' in late Elizabethan culture, 'caused by a collapse of most of the props of the medieval world picture... in England there occurred a phase of unprecedented social and geographical mobility which at the higher levels transformed the composition and size of the gentry and professional classes, and at the lower levels tore hundreds of thousands of individuals loose from their traditional kinship and neighbourhood backgrounds'.[5]

While it is true that English society had inherited the feudal idea of the Great Chain of Being, and with this ideological construct the idea that a static social order was divinely ordained, it is the case that this sort of inherited thinking was also being challenged on many different fronts. In politics, the power of the monarchy and the lords was coming under more democratic pressure to reform. Laws were changing in the same direction; it was in this period that aristocrats settling a dispute via a duel became subject to the common law and ships leaving England for trade and adventure no longer had to carry an aristocrat as part of their crew. Increasing trade was creating a newly prosperous merchant class, especially in London - merchants were growing rich and powerful and upwardly mobile, threatening the established aristocratic class. Science was evolving too from its origins in magic and developing an empirical method that would not just accept inherited understanding of the word, but instead tested evidence objectively via experimentation. At the same time, a range of humanist intellectuals were questioning some of Elizabethan society's fundamental principles. Meanwhile, Puritans were busily decoupling faith in God from loyalty to the church and to the monarch. England may have been relatively peaceful, but it faced the perpetual threat of invasion by Catholic Spain, or France, as well as potential insurrection from within, such as the Earl of Essex's revolt. On top of this,

---

[5] Stone, quoted in Dollimore and Sinfield, *Political Shakespeare*, p.5.

plague had swept through the country in the 1590s and would do so again in 1603. It is within this liminal world of intellectual, religious and cultural turmoil that Othello struggles to find any fixed bearings. Essentially Othello is a throwback to a heroic, chivalric age, but he's living in a modern, commercial and political world. In addition, he is an outsider, a non-European in a sophisticated European capital.

The vision of Elizabethan England as a peaceful golden age is particularly associated in Shakespeare studies with E.M.W. Tillyard and his hugely influential book *The Elizabethan World Picture* [1943] which was, for decades, the core 'background' text on Shakespeare for English Literature undergraduates. In particular, new historicist and cultural materialist criticism starts from the position of rejecting the sort of conservative and nostalgic version of the past Tillyard articulated. As these critics point out, some major historical events undermine Tillyard's rather rose-tinted take on the past. Look backwards a little way from Elizabeths the First's reign and we see political turbulence of the reigns of Henry VIII and his short-lived immediate successors; look forward a couple of years and the Gunpowder Plot of 1605 comes into view, when Catholic conspirators tried to blow up parliament in 1605 and assassinate the king. In addition, cast our eyes a little further forward, and only two decades after Shakespeare had written *Othello* barely suppressed tensions in English society erupted and the country broke into violent civil war. While there is no doubt there were many great achievements of the Elizabethan and Jacobean ages, including Shakespeare's own work, recently historians have exposed the often horrendous experiences of women, ethnic minorities and the poor. Their fine-grained analysis of many different aspects of Late Elizabethan/early Jacobean society reveals it to be a much more unstable, dynamic, dangerous and fascinating age - a maelstrom of clashing ideas and beliefs, or, rather, a cultural furnace that fired Shakespeare's imagination and powered his plays.

Moors and the Ottoman Empire

With the play featuring a threat to the borders of Europe by the Turkish fleet, we might assume that Shakespeare's contemporaries would have harboured hostile feelings towards Moors and the Ottoman Empire. The truth, however, is that their feelings were probably somewhat ambivalent. Attitudes towards Moors were a mixture of fascination as much as fear, as the vogue for the 'Turk play' with its stock character of the exotic foreigner suggests. Elizabethan culture also understood the word 'moor' in a several different ways: Moors were split in the English imagination into 'tawny' North Africans and 'blackamoors' - moors from sub-Saharan Africa, with more hostility generally expressed towards the latter. In addition, the word 'moor' could be understood in a religious rather than racial way, meaning Muslim. Moreover, although the Islamic Ottoman Empire posed a threat to Christian Europe, in 1580 England had entered into a formal contract with the Ottomans, forming a military alliance against the Catholic Church.

Racial theories worried about conversion from one race to another. The climactic theory of race, for instance, posited that a black man would become white in Europe, while other theories suggested that black men would 'infect' white women with black children.

Ania Loomba sums up the racial context of the play helpfully, arguing that the Renaissance marks the beginning of both an opening up to and a closing down against other races. This was period in which the slave trade and colonisation began. Consequently, as a whole, Europeans encountered more people of different ethnicities and cultures. But, while this opened white European eyes to various types of otherness, it also led to racial ideas becoming sedimented in the European psyche.

As the complex history of performances make obvious, Othello is an elusive, composite character, both Moorish and sub-Saharan African, both a slave and also a royal, a Christian, but also a Moor, a black man but one fighting for a white culture. As the 'Moor of Venice', Shakespeare's Othello is a walking, talking cultural and racial contradiction and an extraordinarily bold challenge to contemporary ways of thinking about both race and religion.

Themes

Themes are the dominant ideas repeatedly explored in a text. Shakespeare's plays cover so much ground that they touch on many themes. Concerns of different readers and critics also foreground different themes. For political criticism, for example, themes of power, control and punishment are likely to come to the fore, whereas critics more interested in gender and queer theory might explore the themes of masculine and feminine identity and any fluidity between these unfixed terms. Meanwhile, for postcolonial critics the most pressing themes of *Othello* are its depictions of race, religion and the relationship of a dominant culture to others. As the last of these will be discussed throughout this guide, particularly in our sections on the major characters, we will not explore them separately now.

Faith and belief

Many critics have noted the prominence of religious language in *Othello* and suggested that this reflects the play's engagement with some of the most contentious theological debates of the time. Both principal characters employ religious language, but do so in strikingly different ways: while Iago, who has been likened to a 'blasphemous preacher abusing the ear', employs theological language in a satirical, mocking manner, Othello talks sincerely of the 'eternal soul' of perdition and damnation. As well as expressing concern about the state of his own soul, Othello warns Iago about his and takes great care to try to ensure that Desdemona's soul will be saved before he kills her.

Questions about the nature of faith and of belief are raised in the play most obviously when characters are forced to weigh up evidence and when they do so in very different ways. For example, while some characters privilege what they see, others rely more on the evidence of their ears. Othello claims that he will 'see before' he doubts Desdemona, demands from Iago the 'ocular proof' of his wife's infidelity and believes

---

passionately in the magical properties of the handkerchief, whereas for Desdemona it is merely a valuable piece of cloth. While some characters are easily persuaded to believe something – think of how easily Iago is able to persuade Roderigo that he still has a chance of marrying Desdemona – other characters, such as Lodovico, are less credulous and more demanding of hard facts.

Although the play does not explicitly mention contentious religious debates or seem especially interested in one religion or another, its exploration of the nature of faith and belief reflects many of the acute contemporary concerns about religion circulating in Elizabethan and Jacobean culture. Think, for instance, of how Iago manages to persuade Othello to believe in his evidence of Desdemona's supposed infidelity or the failure of Othello to have faith in the woman he loves.

The immediate context of the play was characterised by religious flux. Having become fully Protestant under the reign of Edward VI [1547-53] England had reverted to Catholicism when Mary I [1553-58] gained the throne. In turn, her successor, Elizabeth I, restored the country to Protestantism and made some reforms to try to accommodate Catholics. However, unhappiness with the treatment of Catholics came to a head under the following monarch, James I, when the gunpowder conspirators sought to blow up parliament in 1605.

Broadly speaking, whereas Catholicism privileges the importance of visual signs, the evidence of the eye, Protestantism emphasised instead the primacy of the word - the evidence of the ear. Indeed, in Shakespeare's lifetime, Protestant reformers declared that belief in the power of sacred relics was superstition and branded as idolatrous the inherited, fundamentally Catholic idea that the world is saturated with sacramental possibilities. For the Protestant reformers, belief in the magical properties of images, signs, tokens, icons meant belief in magic, rather than belief in God's sacred word.

In addition to the division of Christianity into Catholicism and

Protestantism [and also the Eastern Orthodox Church], Protestantism itself had also split into two distinct branches, Calvinism and Lutheranism. The central doctrinal difference between the two branches of Protestantism was that Calvinists believed in predestination [the concept that the elect and the damned have already been chosen by God before birth] whereas Lutheranism held out the hope of heaven to anyone who lived virtuously. This split between the saved and the damned is echoed explicitly in the play when Othello speaks of the sheep and the goats, echoing the famous parable.

Alongside the context of antipathy and fundamental differences about the nature of belief and faith between the Protestants and Catholics, another religion is embroiled in the action of the play. In this period, the Muslim Ottoman Empire was threatening the borders of Christian Europe and in doing so stirring up further profound anxieties about religion, not least fears about conversion, and these are also echoed in the play. For instance, we learn that, despite being consistently labelled as 'the Moor'

 implying he is a Muslim, Othello is a Christian convert – hence his employment of Christian references to damnation and salvation. And this raises awkward questions about the nature and depth of his Christian faith. How, for example, was Othello converted to Christianity? Did this happen when he was taken captive and enslaved? In what circumstances might he turn back to his original faith? Famously, in Laurence Olivier's version of the play, filmed in 1965, Othello tears off his crucifix at a critical moment of violence in Act V, an action that implies that at this point he reverts to an earlier non-Christian version of himself.

As we have noted, Shakespeare does not appear to be interested in any particular religion in *Othello*, not least because he would have been acutely aware of how dangerous it would be to openly question the tenets of any religious faith. *Othello* is certainly, however, an epistemological play, that is, a play profoundly concerned with the basis of knowledge and the nature of proof, with justified or unjustified belief and with the complications of faith. Hot contemporary debates about the role of images and symbols in faith and belief are repeatedly raised in a play that encourages us to think about the meaning of tokens and signs. In short, *Othello* is a play that examines some fundamental epistemological questions: What do we know? What do we think? What are we prepared to believe from that?

Jealousy

The 1995 film of *Othello*, directed by Oliver Parker, was advertised with a caption of four abstract nouns – 'Envy, greed, jealousy and love'. And, although many readers have insisted that racial and cultural issues are at the heart of the tragedy, many others have been as keen to insist that the play is essentially one about universal human emotions and how the power of these can overthrow reason in anyone, however great.

Clearly several of the characters in the play experience jealousy: Roderigo is jealous of Othello's relationship with Desdemona; Iago is jealous of Cassio's promotion and of his courtly qualities and of Othello and his relationship with Desdemona. Most importantly, of course, Othello suffers from the 'green-eyed monster' once he comes to believe his wife has been unfaithful to him. Shakespeare presents jealousy as a kind of torture, an excruciating experience that the sufferer can only find release from through the destruction of its source. Jealousy is essentially disproportionate and twists those who suffer from it into worser selves. Arguably the force of Iago's jealousy drives him to destroy others, while Othello's excessive sexual jealousy makes him blind to Iago's deception as well as to Desdemona's virtues and to the due processes of the law.

The issues of race, identity and jealousy can be linked. Historically some critics argued, for example, that Othello's violent jealousy stemmed from his racial identity and his African heritage. Of course, this racist line of argument can be quickly dismissed. Violent jealousy isn't the preserve of one particular race or another, obviously, and in Shakespeare's own plays, the white Leontes in *The Winter's Tale* suffers from it in a parallel way to

Othello. Jonathan Dollimore puts the opposite case very well when he argues that Othello's jealousy is the corrupted expression of his sense of otherness. Iago, Dollimore opines, seeks to break through Othello's defences in order that his deep social and psychological insecurities will break out, manifested as sexual jealousy, with devastating consequences.

Notably, however, it is male characters in Shakespeare's plays, certainly in *Othello*, who seem to experience excessive sexual jealousy resulting in violence. Perhaps this is because for characters like Othello, the torments of jealousy they experience are intensified by an honour code that sees cheated husbands reduced to monstrous cuckolds. For these men, jealousy becomes impossible to withstand when it is mixed with shame and humiliation.

Justice, Injustice and Prejudice

The theme of justice runs throughout the play. Justice refers to fairness in the way that individuals are treated, by both other individuals and by institutions. In *Othello* characters continually have to face and deal with unfairness and injustice, as a result prejudices against race or gender and from power imbalances.

Throughout Shakespeare's tragedy, prejudice often underpins the unjust ways that characters are treated. Racial prejudice is prominent from the very first scene, as Roderigo and Iago use explicitly racial terms to belittle Othello. Repeatedly identified as other and referred to dismissively as 'the Moor' or by pronouns, rather than by his name, he is dehumanised as a 'Barbary horse' with 'gross clasps' and 'thick lips'. 'Barbary' describes a breed of horse with North African origin, defining Othello as an outsider, marginalised by society, and as someone less human than his white counterparts. In 1601, Queen Elizabeth had complained about what she saw as the proliferation of 'Negars and blackamoors' in her kingdom, and no doubt in Shakespeare times such prejudice was common. The deep-seated, entrenched and seemingly ubiquitous nature of such bigotry rightly shocks a contemporary audience. This discrimination sets the tone for the rest of the play and establishes the injustice that Othello faces as a victim of Iago's manipulative schemes, as well as the disrespect he has to navigate almost everywhere he turns. Meanwhile, in this context, Desdemona and Cassio's lack of prejudice does them both credit.

In addition to racial prejudice, misogyny is rife throughout the play, and Shakespeare focuses on the ways in which women are judged, and condemned, for their 'honesty' and sexuality. Desdemona's fate seems the most unjust and tragic, killed by her jealous husband despite her innocence. Arguably Iago's manipulation of Othello is borne out of his own initial sense of injustice, as Cassio is chosen as Othello's new lieutenant, rather than him. Certainly, Iago's feelings of injustice prompt him to plot the downfall of both Othello and Cassio. At first, however, in contrast, Othello is apparently focused on, and committed to, justice. When faced with Iago's intimations that Desdemona has been unfaithful, Othello demands 'ocular proof' before he will call his 'love a whore'. However, the mood quickly changes, as Othello's commitment to reason and trust of Desdemona vanishes and he is eaten up by jealousy, the 'green-eyed monster', and allows himself to swallow Iago's lies. Tellingly, Othello  uses the language of justice to justify his murder of Desdemona, repeatedly claiming that 'it is the cause'. After kissing her, he sighs, 'O, balmy breath, that dost almost persuade / Justice to break her sword!' How might an actor perform this line? The enjambment and emphatic positioning of the personified 'Justice' suggests that the line would be delivered almost breathlessly, and desperately, emphasising the irony of his call for justice when his own actions are so blatantly – to the audience, at least – unjustified. Othello calls on Desdemona to 'deny each article', further drawing on language of the law to defend what he is doing.

In his final suicide speech, Othello focuses on how he wishes to be remembered, displaying his own internalised prejudices, with descriptions of the 'base Indian and the 'malignant and turban'd Turk' who, echoing the language used at the start of the play about him, Othello animalistically describes as 'the circumcised dog'. His display of racial and religious prejudice here reveals how Othello himself uses his final words not to ask for forgiveness for his murder of his innocent wife but to position himself within dominant Christian society, as he fails to break free from the prejudicial thoughts and behaviours by which he has himself been judged.

Justice does not win. Desdemona is killed; Emilia is killed; Othello kills himself; yet Iago survives. And refuses to justify his actions. Shakespeare's tragedy suggests that individual quests for justice are often the motivation for action – actions that have tragic, irreversible consequences for others. Othello seeks revenge in order to feel as though justice has been served and, in doing so, causes his own downfall as well as the unjust fates of others. In addition, prejudice – particularly racial prejudice and misogyny – is evident from the opening of the play, and remains unchallenged, revealing how dangerous and destructive discrimination can be and the role it plays in the injustices the audience see unravelling on stage.

Masculinity and Military Honour

'Come, be a man', Iago commands of Roderigo in Act I, Scene 3. But, what does it mean to 'be a man', particularly in the world of this play? Throughout *Othello*, male characters seem unshakeably focused on asserting their masculinity and protecting their status and honour. Othello has achieved his status and position through his military prowess and feels fatally undermined in his masculinity when he comes to believe his wife has cuckolded him.

When Cassio falls victim to Iago's manipulative ways, and drunkenly embarrasses himself, it is his 'reputation, reputation, reputation' that he is most concerned about. This repetition highlights how much his status matters to him – without that 'immortal part of [himself]', all that 'remains is bestial'. The paramount importance of honour and status to the men in the play reflects the narrow version of masculinity during the Elizabethan era, one predicated on power and authority, military strength, and a misogynistic attitude towards women and their chasteness and purity. Whilst Othello has built his own status through war, the audience is quickly exposed to the fragility of masculinity and the different ways in which a character's manhood may be questioned, particularly in relation to women. In the first scene, for example, Brabantio's honour is called into question by Iago and Roderigo due to the fact that his daughter, Desdemona, has fallen in love with Othello and shows 'obedience' to him rather than to her father.

As the play continues, we see how Iago pushes Othello to question his masculinity by making him worry about how much control he really has of Desdemona. What had seemed to be a relationship of stable love in Act I [albeit one where Othello still needed to assert that Desdemona 'loved [him] for the dangers [he] had pass'd'], quickly turns unstable and sour as the misplaced handkerchief provides Othello with the [false] evidence he demanded to believe Desdemona has been unfaithful. He strikes her and uses derogatory gendered language, belittling her as nothing more than an 'Impudent strumpet!' Defining Desdemona by her sexuality, he likens her to a brazen prostitute because his own sense of masculinity has been so undermined. Rather than believe his wife or Emilia, Othello trusts his fellow man, too quickly falling for Iago's lies, and feels the need to punish Desdemona through murder, using the same sort of violence and ruthlessness he has demonstrated at war.

The anxious masculinity that Othello displays in so easily believing Iago's lies about Desdemona's betrayal leads him to end her life. He describes himself as 'honourable' in his murder, and claims he would be 'damn'd beneath all depth of hell' but for the fact that he 'did proceed upon just grounds'. This self-justification is steeped in patriarchal ideals, as Othello believes himself right to condemn Desdemona for his 'honour', and only questions 'why should honour outlive honesty' once Emilia reveals the truth about the handkerchief – that she gave it to her husband and

Desdemona was nothing but faithful to Othello.

Iago, too, displays his craving for honour and an anxiety about his masculinity. His desire for Othello's validation, by being promoted to lieutenant, is one prompt for his plotting to bring about Othello's downfall. His criticism of Cassio, successfully appointed to the position of lieutenant above him, is riddled with misogynistic language: Cassio is no 'More than a spinster', Iago claims, and his first act of revenge is to 'shame' Brabantio in telling him about Desdemona's love for Othello, using sexually demeaning language to mock Othello. Within the military setting of the opening scene, there is another war waging – Iago's battle for revenge.

The play ends with a focus on Othello's fragile masculinity. He entreats that he has 'done the state some service', listing his military achievements, afraid that he may not be remembered for his physical strength and bravery on the battlefield. Whilst the audience sees the strength of the female characters, for instance through Desdemona's own rhetoric and Emilia's courage to stand up to Iago and defend her mistress' honour, we also see the devastating consequences of narrow definitions of masculinity and how the need to prove one's honour and manhood can override rationality, emotional awareness and open-mindedness.

Shakespeare's language

In the 1930s a literary academic, Caroline Spurgeon, wrote a hugely influential critical study of Shakespeare's language, called *Shakespeare's Imagery and What it Tells Us*. The central idea of Spurgeon's study was that Shakespeare's figurative imagery falls into groups or clusters and these clusters vary from play to play. Moreover, Spurgeon opined that these image clusters are the most important generators of the distinct mood and atmosphere of each play as well as also conveying key thematic concerns. For instance, we might quickly think of the multiple images of animals in *Macbeth*. Like *King Lear*, the Scottish play houses a menagerie of creatures, from poor 'wrens' and 'mewing' cats to 'hell-kites', a 'Russian bear' and even an 'armed rhinoceros'. *Hamlet* rivals these two tragedies in terms of the number and range of animals used in imagery, from Osric as a water-fly to a crocodile Hamlet claims he could eat to show the depth of his love for the dead Ophelia. Spurgeon's approach is, as you can see, incisive, allowing us to fillet each play for the seemingly richest cuts of language.

However, since the 1930s her approach has been refined and refined in various ways. There are three main criticisms, the first of which is less obvious, the other two probably a bit more predictable: as a pioneering female literary academic writing in the 1930s, Spurgeon was constrained by ladylike decorum and hence she entirely ignored sexual imagery. Critics have also contested her choices of image clusters in each play, suggesting that alternative clusters are just as significant or even more so. Other critics have gone a step further, disagreeing with the privileging of imagery above other linguistic features. Why, for instance, is imagery more significant than repeated single words [think of the importance of 'honest' in *Othello*] or other literary devices such as antithesis and doubling language ['I am not what I am']? What about the use of verse, and prose, and Shakespeare's bending and meshing of iambic pentameter with syntax? What about rhetorical devices? Some critics have identified hendiadys as the key language technique in *Othello*. And beyond linguistic devices, aren't characters also pretty important, especially in a text that is written to be performed by actors on a stage? Words, of course, matter, but there's an old cliché that actions speak louder. And so the debates go on... No doubt there's a literary academic out there somewhere who'd argue that the real key to unlocking Shakespeare's plays is the playwright's use of prepositions or conjunctions. If that's you, then, please do get in touch and explain how your theory works...

Image clusters in *Othello*
Animals and beasts

Probably, when we mentioned animal imagery in Shakespeare's other great tragedies, some similar images from *Othello* immediately sprung to mind. How many images of animals can you recall without referring to the text? From the top or our heads, there's the 'old black ram' and 'Barbary horse', the 'white ewe', Desdemona as a hunting hawk and as disgustingly polluted, like a 'cistern, for foul toads', Othello himself not wanting to be like a toad and being led 'like an ass' by the nose by Iago. Added to that Iago describes Cassio as a great 'fly' to be trapped in his web of intrigue and Desdemona's singing is described as capable of soothing the 'savageness out of a bear'. Othello refers to sheep and goats and, in exasperation, to goats and monkeys. Meanwhile, Cassio calls Bianca a 'fitchew', a kind of polecat. Check the text and you'll find other animals, with references to cats, a guinea-hen, blind puppies, a swan and perhaps most surprisingly, a baboon.

When applied to the characters this imagery is obviously debasing and dehumanising. It implies that under the surface, human beings are really no more civilised or noble or good or loving than dumb beasts, that we are driven more by base appetites than we are by fine principles and values. Which character holds and promulgates this contemptuous and cynical view of human beings and of society? Iago, of course. Overwhelmingly the animal imagery in the play is used by Iago. The distinguished critic G. Wilson Knight argued in 1930 that Othello speaks, contrastingly, in a lovely, lyrical, almost hypnotic way, a style Wilson Knight dubbed the 'Othello music'. It is a poignant part of the tragedy that Iago manages to infect and pollute this music to such an extent that Othello begins to use the same animalistic

———

imagery of contempt and disgust, even about himself.

A step further away from humans are the unnatural animals, the beasts and monsters, in the play, such as 'the green-eyed monster' of jealousy, the image of a husband turned into the monstrous 'horned man', the cuckold, and of Desdemona as a 'white devil'. Some critics suggest that as the play progresses the animals mentioned become increasingly more monstrous.

Blackness and whiteness

Unsurprisingly, some of the animalistic imagery also uses the binary colour imagery of black and white. From the examples cited, for instance, there's  Othello as an 'old black ram' and the 'fair' Desdemona as a 'white devil'. The colour imagery in the play engages with contemporary ideas about race, religion and gender. In the Jacobean period, whiteness was not only associated with purity and virtue but also with Christianity, whereas blackness was associated with Islam as well as with evil, corruption and danger. The play raises awkward questions about a series of relationships, not only between white and black or goodness and evil, but also between whiteness and evil and blackness and Christianity. For example, was it possible during the Renaissance to be a black person and also to be a good Christian? Are Iago's evil deeds the result of his warped humanity or a toxic product of white, Christian Venice?

Kim F. Hall has suggested that during the early modern period darkness and lightness became a vehicle through which the English could begin to construct ideas of 'self' and 'other', with whiteness construed as good and self and blackness as evil and 'other'. Taking this idea on, some critics have focused on the interplay of the black and white imagery in Othello to suggest that the frequently antithetical relationship between the two colours expresses a fear of miscegenation, the mixing of races to produce mixed race offspring. Certainly, early critics were not disgusted so much by Shakespeare making the noble hero black, but by the idea of his relationship with Desdemona's whiteness and maidenly purity. Anxiety about interracial mingling has been felt acutely too by some audiences, such as those during Apartheid in South Africa and in the U.S.A. during segregation, as the infamous story of a nineteenth-century American audience member shooting the actor playing Othello suggests.

Patricia Parker has explored how racialised language of colour is used with reference to the female characters. Iago tells us, for example, that he intends to blacken Desdemona's name, by turning her 'virtue' into 'pitch'. Meanwhile, Shakespeare seems to deliberately undermine contemporary racial ideas of virtue and sin by making a character called Bianca, which directly translates to 'white', a prostitute.

Of course, a terrible and poignant feature of the play is how Iago corrupts Othello's mind to such an extent that even he begins to use racial stereotypes. As Kiernan Ryan notes, Othello eventually views his marriage to Desdemona 'through white Venetian eyes and in white Venetian terms' showing how 'deeply he has absorbed the entrenched prejudice of Venetian culture'. The most notorious example of this, of course, is the pejorative simile Othello uses about Desdemona in Act III, Sc. 3:

'Her name, that was fresh / As Dian's visage, is now begrimed and black / as my own face.'

In this horribly tormented image, Othello sees himself and his own colour not as a symbol or strength or purity, but as dirty and as a symbol of corruption.

Appearance and reality

If there's one image cluster predominant in Shakespeare's work as a whole this one might well be it. And we might pause to wonder why Shakespeare seems so obsessed with ontological[6] and metaphysical issues. Arguably, it's because of the nature of plays themselves. Pretending, acting and putting on

---

[6] Concerning the nature of reality.

masks are inherent features of drama texts in a fundamental way that is not true of poetry or novels. The Romantic poet, Samuel Taylor Coleridge, wrote about audiences' willing suspension of disbelief when we watch plays. Obviously, when watching *Othello* in a theatre, on one level we know that we are in a theatre and not really in Venice or Cyprus. Even with films, where directors can create a stronger sense of verisimilitude, we still know we are watching through a screen and that the characters depicted are not real people and are being played by actors. And, yet, for films and especially for plays to fully cast their spell on us, we have to let ourselves go with the spectacle, fill in the blanks with our imaginations, take what we see to be real, at least for the duration of the performance.

In other words, ontological or more broadly metaphysical issues, issues concerning what is real and what is pretence, what seems to be and what actually is, are the essence of theatre, and especially so for plays that are highly literary – written, for instance, in iambic pentameter – and yet want us to feel as we watch them as if the characters and actions are absolutely real.

Of course, from the outset, the confusion of what is real with what is false is integral to *Othello*. Moreover, this confusion is a deliberate strategy of deception, delivered by Iago. In the first scene, Iago is trying to deceive Brabantio about the nature of his daughter's relationship with Othello. Simultaneously, Iago is also deceiving Roderigo in presenting himself as helping him to achieve his aim of marrying Desdemona, and soon after deceiving Othello about the nature of his relationship with Roderigo. Of course, Iago will also deceive everyone else, including Othello and deceive his master into thinking his wife has been unfaithful to him. From the start of the play, deception is also mirrored by the threat of the Turkish fleet, which appears to be making preparation to attack Rhodes. However, as the senate realise, his preparation is just a false show, a 'pageant' to keep them in 'false gaze'.

Confine yourself to just the first act and you'll find several images of deception. For example, while speaking to Roderigo, in scene 1, Iago refers to servants who only pretend to be loyal to masters to serve their own ends.

These are servants who though 'trimmed in forms and visages of duty' and 'throwing but shows of service on their lords... do themselves homage'. Indeed, he admits he is one of these, so that 'following' Othello he really 'follow but myself'. Ironically, given the nature of his relationship with Roderigo, Iago also warns his dupe that 'I am not what I am'. Notably in these constructions, antithesis is used to contrast how people appear to be and how they really are, and in the latter two the mirroring language ['following' / 'follow'' 'I am' / 'not what I am'] suggests it will often be very difficult for other characters to make out the one from the other. Meanwhile, stung by the discovery that Desdemona has left him Brabantio warns fathers to 'trust not your daughters' minds / By what you see them act'.

Though Iago is the arch deceiver, Desdemona and women in general are accused of deception. Much later in the play, Iago will undermine Othello's trust of his wife by suggesting that all Venetian wives are essentially untrustworthy and should not be judged on their appearances: 'In Venice, they do let God see the Pranks / They dare not show their husbands.' Infected by Iago's poison, Othello, of course, comes to believe his wife is 'false as water' and in several memorable images conveys his disgust at her apparent deception. For instance, he calls her a 'cunning' and 'subtle whore', a 'closet lock and key of villainous secrets', whose kneeling and prayers are just a pretence of piousness. In another image of the same thought, although she seems 'so lovely fair, and smell'st so sweet / That the sense aches at thee', she is really a 'weed'. Agonisingly, in the final scene, Othello is still struggling to equate Desdemona's apparent fairness with her apparent villainy. Her pure, white skin is, for instance, as 'smooth as monumental alabaster', the 'cunning'st pattern of excelling nature'. Here, again he thinks of her as a 'rose', not a 'weed', as if it would only take the very slightest alteration in his thoughts to see her goodness, realise his mistake and not murder her.

Minor Image Clusters

Other repeated patterns of images include those of transformation, of hunting and catching, of commerce and of carnal appetites and sexual disgust. For example, Othello's seduction of Desdemona is described by her father as a kind of black magic, Iago talks of using a 'net' to entrap his victims and

---

Desdemona is compared to a hunting hawk. Iago's repeated injunction to Roderigo to put money in his purse reflects a shift in societal values, with money replacing loyalty and duty as the basis for service. Similarly, the language of commerce and property is used especially about the women in the play – Brabantio is 'robbed' of Desdemona; Cassio refers to Bianca dismissively as a 'bauble', whereas Desdemona is a 'jewel', characterised finally by Othello as a 'pearl'.

Both Iago and, under his influence, Othello express disgust about sex. Olfactory imagery is used specially to convey the visceral effect of Iago's pornographic imaginings of congress between Othello and Desdemona: 'Fie, one may smell in such, a will most rank'. Is there a puritanical disgust of sex itself here or is the disgust caused by the nature of the lovers? Indeed, bearing in mind how often appearances are deceptive in the play, does Iago actually feel any disgust himself or is his language calculated to cause powerful revulsion in his hearers?

Verse and prose

As we have noted, Othello's language is characteristically grand and lyrical. [Indeed, some critics have suggested it is rather self-consciously so.] The beauty and grandeur of the 'Othello music' expresses the qualities of his inner nature and the verse Othello speaks, even under duress at the start of the play, is the outward manifestation of his inner confidence. Hence any collapse into prose on his behalf is more powerful and dramatic through contrast. Compare the calm and measured quality of this, from Act 1, sc. 3:

'Most potent, grave and reverend signors,
My very noble and approved good masters
That I have ta'en away this old man's daughter,
It is most true; true I have married her:
The very head and from of my offending
Hath this extent, no more.'

to the following passage, from Act IV, Sc.1:

'Lie with her? Lie on her? We say lie on her when they belie her! Lie with her, zounds, that's fulsome! – Handkerchief! Confessions! Handkerchief! – To confess and be hanged for his labour! First to be hanged, and then to confess: I tremble at it. Nature would not invest herself in such shadowing passion without some instruction. It is not words that shakes me thus. Pish! Noses, ear, and lips. Is't possible? Confess! Handkerchief! O devil!'

Whereas in the first example one coherent thought unfolds evenly and smoothly, underpinned by the regular iambic pentameter, in the second Othello's language is reduced to a staccato volley of confounded questions and exclamations. There is no metre, of course, and at times syntax also gives way, so that Othello is reduced to spluttering single words. Emotions are mixed with thinking, ideas and words are repeated and the overall impression is of disorder and distress. As Simon Palfrey vividly describes it in *Doing Shakespeare*, Othello's language here 'chugs and stutters like a dying engine into stasis', with the 'collapse out of iambic control' anticipating his loss not only of self-control but of his sense of himself.

We have mentioned earlier how Iago pollutes Othello's imagination and poisons the 'Othello music'. Here is another way in which Iago infects and degrades Othello's language. For it is Iago who is the dominant speaker of prose in the play. He speaks in prose with Roderigo and with Cassio, sometimes even with Desdemona. Though rarely does he try it on with Othello. Indeed, adept as ever at changing his language to suit his purpose and audience, Iago can employ the regularity of metre to make his weasel words sound convincing. As the actor Simon Bubb has pointed out, Iago's fake naïve lines from the opening of Act 4 describing Desdemona's actions are in perfect iambic pentameter:

'Or to be naked with her friend in bed
An hour or more, not meaning any harm?'

They work perfectly on Othello, in whose incredulous response the metre goes tellingly off the rails:

'Naked in bed, Iago, and not mean harm!'

Words, words, words

As in all of Shakespeare's work, certain key words crop up over and over again in *Othello*. These words also appear sometimes in groups, as synonyms with similar meanings. We don't mean commonly used function words such as 'I' or 'and', but rather meaning-carrying words, mainly nouns, verbs and adjectives. Tracking who uses these echoing words and when and whether the meanings they ascribe to them, i.e. their semantics, are stable or change with speaker or time or place is an incisive way of mapping the major concerns of the play. Think, for example, of how Iago's use of the simple verb 'to be' establishes the play's focus on identity and deception: 'I am not what I am'.

Sometimes when the same words are used in very close proximity, they can generate a sense of obsessive, almost torturous concentration. In his conversation with Othello about Cassio in Act III, for instance, Iago weaves together the words 'think' and 'know' in order to undermine Othello's confidence in his own perceptions. Adding to the web are other key words, such as 'honest', 'shown' and 'seem', that allude to the tricky business of distinguishing between outer appearances and reality. The repetition of these words expresses a central concern of the play and an increasing problem for Othello – how can we know anything for sure?

Single words are also used as epithets - as a kind of shorthand to describe characters. Obviously and ironically, of course, the epithet 'honest' sticks to Iago like glue, while Desdemona is often described as 'sweet' and at the start of play, the Duke admiringly refers to 'valiant Othello'.

Critical commentaries

1. Shakespeare wrote all his plays using a five Act structure, right?
2. Usually the middle Act, Act III is pivotal with the action of the first two Acts building up to this and the action of the following two Acts revealing the consequences of action taken in this Act, right?

Well, not exactly. Actually, although the scene divisions are his, Shakespeare wrote no plays at all using the famous five Act structure. This was a structure imposed on his plays long after he was dead, in the 1720s by the editor Nicholas Rowe. Nevertheless, it is true that many of Shakespeare's plays build towards a midpoint which functions like a pivot and that in modern editions this pivotal usually occurs in scenes now labelled as taking place in Act III.

How many scenes are there in the play in total? How many scenes are there in each act of *Othello*? Which Act is longest, which the shortest? Which scene is the longest and which the shortest? When and where are the soliloquies placed? How many scenes feature Iago? How many scenes show female characters talking to each other without the presence of men? Time spent mapping out these details helps to focus critical attention on the structure of Shakespeare's play.

As well as providing a broad overview of the major content of each scene therein, the following commentaries also include some close analysis of short passages from within each act. These sections exemplify the sort of close reading of the drama that is both enriching and often a part of assessment at both GCSE and A-level.

Act I

As in all his great tragedies, Shakespeare plunges us straight into the story unprepared, a master of *in media res* storytelling. In *Macbeth* we are dropped into sinister, witchy intrigue; in *Hamlet* we eavesdrop on anxious, ghost-rattled sentries; in *King Lear* we join the swirl of courtly whispers as the king divides his kingdom with great pomp. *Othello* begins, significantly, at night and with the antagonist Iago's bitter complaints. There is no pedestrian preparation

here; instead we dive into a narrative current that carries us swiftly along with great, if confusing, momentum. Roderigo, Iago's dupe and pawn, states irascibly that 'I take it much unkindly that [...] thou shouldst know this'. The nature of this *this* is not immediately apparent, so the audience must listen into this conspiratorial conversation to learn more. The instant we lean in, Shakespeare has us: we listen avidly to try to find our bearings in the story.

In a mere 30 lines Shakespeare establishes quickly both a motivation for Iago's antagonism and also his relationship with Roderigo. We learn quickly that Iago is paid by Roderigo ['thou hast had my purse as if the strings were thine'] but what exactly is he paying him for? Is this a relationship of exploitation or one of symbiosis? Again, what's going on here is shrouded in murky mystery. What is not a mystery is the fact that Iago hates 'him'. This 'him,' of course, is not named initially but we learn quickly that this person is Iago's superior and, in a 26-line speech that radiates bitterness and injured pride, has passed over Iago for promotion. What is particularly notable is that the 'him' who has slighted Iago so painfully is only bitingly described as 'his Moorship', a crucial clue, and this only at the end of Iago's rant.

So what? What Iago does here essentially dehumanises this person by defining him strictly through his racial character, refusing to name him and denying him a name and a humanity. Iago's sarcastic addressing of royalty, 'his Moorship,' points to Othello's status and origins, a man from North Africa, usually dark-skinned and of Muslim faith. In fact, Othello, the 'him' in question, is not specifically named until Act I, Sc. 3, despite appearing on stage in Sc. 2. Repeatedly, the other characters refer to him as 'the Moor', which points to an unusual protagonist for the play. Compared to the military hero in *Macbeth*, the intellectual prince in *Hamlet* and the ageing king in *King Lear*, Othello is not *a* Moor among many but *the* only one – he is very much an outsider figure in the social world he moves in.

But what exactly is Iago's gripe and is it justified? Othello has promoted 'One Michael Cassio, a Florentine that never set a squadron in the field' to the position of 'lieutenant' and made Iago 'his ancient', a type of lowly ensign or standard-bearer. Though also an outsider in Venice, Cassio is given a name, presumably because he's white. Iago has his clear reasons for feeling aggrieved: Cassio is inexperienced, a theoretical soldier rather than a practical man: 'mere prattle without practice is all his soldiership'. Note the harsh cacophony of this description, with its aggressive Ps, Ts and Cs, that reinforces Iago's disgust as he bemoans how his extensive experience 'at Rhodes, at Cyprus and on other grounds' is devalued. To Iago, Cassio's promotion smacks of one outsider looking after another. Iago cannot understand Othello's inability to recognise his suitability for promotion. Othello's 'eyes had seen the proof' yet he denies what's obvious, a subtle suggestion of the tragedy to come. Othello is blind to reality and makes disastrous choices like a man lost in fog. Unfortunately, for Othello, the fog which destroys him is man-made.

We quickly learn Iago's not to be trusted - he's a two-faced trickster as his swearing to the Roman god Janus [a two-faced deity] in Sc 2. signals. He's shown to have reasons for how he acts and, crucially, the means to get what

 he wants. Chillingly, he declares that 'I am not what I am,' a warning that dozy Roderigo completely misses. Unfortunately, Roderigo has not connected paying Iago [to achieve another murky, unspecified end] with Iago's explanation that 'I follow him (Othello) to serve my turn upon him'. Iago's a user and an arch manipulator of people and Roderigo is taken in by him as much as anyone. In the rush to take in everything that's going on, it's easy for the audience to miss how explicitly Iago tells us he is duplicitous and not to be trusted. After all, Roderigo's there and he misses it. But with hindsight, it is easy to spot. But then hindsight is all very well after the event. Just ask Othello. It's almost as if Iago is flaunting his villainy, waving it in Roderigo's face, but the fool's so intent on securing his own desires that he doesn't stop to think Iago might also be serving his turn upon *him*.

Iago also establishes himself as a fleet-witted schemer, a quality which becomes ever more evident and frighteningly impressive as the play progresses. An opportunist for turning situations to his advantage, he is the one who declares that they should 'call up her father'. Another minor mystery. Who is he talking about? Why is this woman's father going to be useful to them? Why exactly are they going to 'poison his delight' 'with like timorous accent'? Again, the expert storyteller, Shakespeare knows we will wait to find out more and anticipate the growing tension when Iago and Roderigo begin their antics.

The vague actions of this pair swiftly come into focus: Othello has eloped with the daughter of the man whose sleep they are disturbing, and he seems completely unaware of his daughter's actions. More questions spring to mind: why did Othello and this daughter need to elope? Why is Roderigo involved in all this when he has nothing to do with Othello? Why does Iago take a shadowy backseat when it was he who ordered Roderigo to 'call up her father'? Why does their language descend into outright racism? Some speculative answers: the father, Brabantio, must not approve of the marriage [because Othello's a Moor?]; Roderigo owes Iago something possibly or he is plotting against Brabantio's father. Iago is a master of allowing others to take the action he desires, so much so that he is often referred to as a type of ruthless puppeteer; he agitates and provokes others into rash actions. Hence, the provocative racist language used to animate Roderigo and bait Brabantio. On stage, the taunting of Brabantio usually sees Iago hidden in shadow or behind some object that conceals his identity, while Roderigo is usually bathed in light, in giddy delight at his opportunity to provoke.

Iago shrewdly manipulates others into responding emotionally rather than logically, thus maximising the potential for chaotic mistakes. While using language like 'the thicklips' to describe Othello highlights the disdain of the two men towards the tragic hero, telling Brabantio that 'even now, now, very

now, an old black ram is tupping your white yew' aims to inflame the situation. The stabbing, frantic rhythm of these lines conveys their assault on decency, encouraging Brabantio to visualise in no uncertain terms 'your daughter and the Moor [...] making the beast with two backs'. Subtle it ain't, but highly effective it is, especially when Shakespeare has Brabantio already having dreamt of this: 'this accident is not unlike my dream, belief of it oppresses me already'. Tellingly, Iago piles on the vulgarities, allows Roderigo to take over then scuttles off before meeting Brabantio face-to-face. His use of 'ram,' 'Barbary horse' and 'beast' presents Othello as animalistic and the marriage itself as based in animal desires and lust. Othello and his new wife are holed up in 'the Saggitary,' a lowly inn unbecoming to a senator's daughter and significantly symbolised by the sign of Sagittarius, the Centaur. Half-man, half-horse, this mythical creature represents seething animal lusts and general beastly behaviour, the type that Iago so vividly conjures up for Brabantio. Roderigo's pointing to Othello's 'gross clasps' and 'lascivious' nature aggravates the matter even further. His description of the elopement as a 'gross revolt' and Othello as 'an extravagant and wheeling stranger of here and everywhere' reinforces it as unnatural and disgusting, fired by the hysterical myth of the black male predator feeding off innocent white women. Roderigo's enthusiasm for besmirching Othello's reputation is also made clear as it becomes obvious that he has been rejected by Brabantio as a suitor: 'my daughter is not for thee'.

To rewind a little, though… before Iago exits this world of half-lights and half-truths, he reveals that we won't just be dealing with explosive sexual politics but also more wide-ranging geopolitics: Othello is about to be 'embarked with such loud reason to the Cyprus wars'. The promise of exciting personal conflict between Othello and his aggrieved father-in-law is echoed by an even more exciting promise: the clash of civilisations and of pitched battle. Shame it never happens though: spoiler alert; it's just one long tease on that front!

Before we glide into Act I, Sc. 2 we have already heard a lot about our titular hero, but have yet to meet him. It is an excellent way to build audience anticipation on Shakespeare's part, but it also exemplifies a wider strategy of Iago's mischief-making. Othello's identity is refracted through the words and opinions of others: Iago's embittered entitlement, Roderigo's jealous covetousness or Brabantio's horrified helplessness. Already before we meet Othello, his character and reputation have been distorted, refracted through the self-serving lenses of others. Even his voice is recounted by Iago: 'for 'Certes,' says he, 'I have already chose my officer''. Therefore, as we meet Iago and Othello outside the Sagittary, we wait with a heightened curiosity to test repute against actuality, something Othello dismally fails to do himself in the play.

He cuts an impressive figure, all in all. In contrast to the storm of jealousy and fear that boils up out of the darkness in Act I Sc. 1, Othello proves calm and controlled, a natural commander, seeming authoritative and confident in his own powerful status as military leader of the Venetians. In the face of Iago's warning about Brabantio's 'potential as double as the duke's' Othello is moored [pun intended] in the esteem of his own success, reflected in his assured, almost glib, reply for Brabantio to 'do his spite'. This is not a man easily frightened or even ruffled. In contrast to all the talk of his animalistic unnaturalness, he is reasonable [''tis better as it is'[, articulate ['my services, which I have done the signiory, shall out-tongue his complaints'] yet direct and straight-talking ['I love the gentle Desdemona']. Notably, rather than speed off to the Duke's council, as requested, he goes inside to talk to his new wife, a sign of his equal valuing of his love and his martial responsibility: 'I will but spend a word here in the house'.

However, despite Othello's gravitas and goodness, there is something unnerving about the dramatic irony of watching Iago lie so blatantly to his face and Othello taking these words at face value. In fact, it is a dramatic strategy that Shakespeare uses extremely well. Throughout the entire play, Iago speaks seven soliloquies to Othello's three, which places the audience in an extremely uncomfortable position: we are both unwilling accomplices in Iago's blackguarding and also helpless bystanders in Othello's ruination. Watching Iago's smooth duplicity can be agonising at times as we see him say one thing, while knowing he feels and desires something completely different. And, although we must feel morally appalled by Iago, isn't part of us intrigued to see how his machinations will play out? It is telling that Iago knows about the Cyprus situation before Othello does.

More immediately threatening is the confrontation with Brabantio. Othello handles a potentially violent confrontation with great ease and, it must be said, respect. His calm is a foil to Brabantio's shuddering outrage, which was exactly as Iago had planned it. When Othello implores them to 'keep up your bright swords, for the dew will rust them' it can be delivered with tones of firm authority or more jovial placation. Othello's placatory advice that 'you shall more command with years than with your weapons,' where he is careful to use the respectful 'you' pronoun, contrasts starkly with Brabantio's raging 'O thou foul thief, where hast thou stowed my daughter?' Brabantio's use of 'thou'

reinforces his view that he's speaking to a social inferior, while his use of apostrophe suggests the intense emotions he struggles to control. His 20-line complaint, full of furious disbelief, continues the motif of dehumanising language to describe Othello: he fumes that it is impossible his daughter would shun 'the wealthy, curled darlings of our nation [and] run to the sooty bosom of such a thing as thou'. Desperately,  almost laughably, he declares that only 'foul charms [...or] drugs' could lead to such a disgusting union. Othello knows there is no reasoning with a madman, so wisely suggests they discuss it with the duke who has called them both to 'council'. This authoritative calm is a complete foil to Brabantio's racist fury. When Othello asks Brabantio 'where will you that I go to answer this your charge?' Brabantio's reply of 'to prison' is almost ludicrous.

Similarly to what has happened with Othello in Act I, Sc. 1, we hear about Desdemona before we meet her, another shrewd use of audience anticipation to keep us leaning into the play's narrative. But by the end of Act I Sc. 2, we have heard first, then measured second the character of Othello and he has impressed, rendering Iago's complaints about him invalid, gossipy and malicious. Our trust in Iago must siphon away, making him a mere malcontent, a common figure in Shakespearean drama [see Edmund in *King Lear*, Don John in *Much Ado About Nothing* or Malvolio in *Twelfth Night* as examples]. And we know for sure he is a man not to be trusted. Michael Cassio is also shown to us and even though we cannot measure his soldiership, we can admire his efficiency and discretion. He seems either to misunderstand or tactfully ignore Iago's crude sexual innuendo about how Othello 'tonight hath boarded a land carrack.' He appears to know nothing of the elopement, but this is highly unlikely as later Othello claims Cassio knew everything about his courtship of Desdemona. So, he must be trying to respect the privacy of his commander and also to damp down the type of crude gossip that Iago tries to stoke up.

Two short scenes have hurtled by, creating all types of emotional intensity and skilful, light-touch exposition to get us to Act I, Sc. 3. This is the key scene in Act I, and also the longest. Here we meet Desdemona in the flesh and also see the lovers on stage together for the first time. Again, we are plunged into the middle of a conversation. The duke is busily conferring with his councillors. Into the chaos and 'heat' of this discussion bursts dramatically another form of chaos, Brabantio roaring for personal justice in the midst of a larger geopolitical storm. For the duke, this is awkward in the extreme. He has bigger fish to fry than some love squabble. Plus, he needs his most trusted commander to be battle-ready and fighting invading Turks not fighting an irate father-in-law.

Notably, Othello here is defined by his character, specifically his courage, with the adjective 'valiant' used twice to describe him. No 'lascivious' or 'sooty bosom' or 'black ram'. The most powerful man in Venice, the duke, is the first person to refer to Othello directly by name in the play, suggesting the high esteem he holds him in. The duke is careful to placate Brabantio, an important senator, while also being even-handed to both sides. When Brabantio reveals the 'criminal' responsible for stealing away his daughter to be 'this Moor' the war council's unified response - 'we are sorry for't' - is highly ambiguous. It can simply mean they are sorry for his grievance, sorry for the fact that this has occurred between two important men or, probably more realistically, they are sorry that this had to happen *now*, of all times. They need Othello, and they need him now and the situation renders Brabantio's genuine complaint as slightly hysterical, trivial even, in the face of greater political problems.

While Brabantio's account is full of wild language like 'abused,' 'corrupted,' 'preposterously' and 'witchcraft', Othello's addressing of the war council is respectful and transparent, neither evasive nor emotional. It sounds like a thoughtful speech in its respect to his social superiors: 'most potent, grace and reverend signiors, my very noble and approved good masters'. Othello claims that 'rude am I in my speech and little blest with the soft phrase of peace,' something that appears true when he bluntly states that 'I have ta'en away this old man's daughter'. Hardly a subtle way of calming the matter down. But is this claim true? Does he really talk like a soldier in functional, spare language? His lyrical request for the warring clans in Act I Sc. 2 to 'keep up your bright swords, for the dew will rust them' would suggest he has a gift for elaborate, beautiful language. Certainly, until Iago turns his love to burning jealousy, Othello's language can be elegant and beautiful, an outward expression of his inner peace and, arguably, his essentially noble nature.

Moreover. Othello's aim to tell the story of his courtship, from his perspective, reveals a tendency to tell it straight, the exact opposite of Iago. The opposite, in fact, to Iago's proclamation in Act I Sc. 1 that he would 'not wear' his 'heart upon' his 'sleeve for daws to peck at'. Whereas Iago spends most of the play twisting or hiding the truth and covering his real emotions and motivation, Othello's tragedy, like the great Oedipus, is to spend most of the time trying to uncover the truth and destroying himself in the process. Othello insists on telling his side of the society scandal that is his marriage: 'I will a round, unvarnished tale deliver of my whole course of love'. Brabantio's insistence on Desdemona's naivety as a sheltered ingenue ['a maiden never bold, of spirit so still and quiet that motion blushed at herself'] is so superlative that it can only be wish-fulfilment, rather than fact: Actually, Desdemona is waiting for Othello in The Sagittary inn and Othello appears a noble, respected and, crucially, truthful man. Brabantio's tirade is notable too for projecting a type of hidden societal attitude towards outsiders like Othello onto his daughter: 'she, in spite of nature, of years, of country, of credit, everything to fall in love

 with what she feared to look on?' In his fury and grief, he reveals that an interracial marriage between a sophisticated Venetian woman and a Moor, no matter how 'valiant,' was considered perverse, 'against all rules of nature'. Perhaps Brabantio is just saying what everyone else feels but dare not say. More optimistically, perhaps not everyone in Venice shares his racist attitude. Several other significant characters, including the most authoritative one present, the head of the Venetian state, the duke, as well as the noble Florentine, Cassio, do not seem to have any problem at all in accepting an interracial marriage. Nevertheless, the racial discrimination that has been present from the very start explodes from a private dispute out into a very public forum. This could get ugly, but the duke acts justly and wisely to diffuse the tension.

The vitriol of Brabantio's words reveals that the duke has an unwanted situation on his hands when he needs to get on with more important business. Note Lodovico's subtle reframing of the argument, suggesting that Brabantio's accusations that Othello's blackness brings with it a type of black magic are not credible. He reduces Brabantio's complaints to 'thin habits' and 'poor likelihoods'. Sensing the subtle change in alliance, a senator encourages Othello to redress the balance of Brabantio's skewed version of events: 'But, Othello, speak'. Rather surprisingly, Othello, decides not to speak, but instead allows his brand-new wife to tell her side of the story, to hear her truth uncorrupted by his affections… but then goes on and tells his story while we await her arrival anyway! While this makes no real sense it does two things dramatically speaking: it creates a) suspense as we wait for her and b) allows Shakespeare to engineer a confrontation between an overbearing father and his errant daughter.

To kill time, while Iago fetches Desdemona, Othello fills us in. His claim that 'her father loved me, oft invited me' sounds dubious in the heat of Brabantio's racist attacks on his character, an ominous sign that Othello fails to read much further than surface impressions of people. Shakespeare takes this opportunity to quickly fill in Othello's backstory, painting an inspirational journey from 'being taken by the insolent foe and sold to slavery' to his 'redemption' as a man of military prowess. It is a glamorous, exotic tale, almost mythical or self-mythologising, and this suggests more truthfully the 'love' of Brabantio for Othello as an entertaining freak, an exotic, fascinating other. For Desdemona, though, the storyteller, not the stories, is the fascination: 'she loved me for the dangers I passed and I loved her that she did pity them,' which sounds fine, until you examine it more closely. It's hardly the stuff of soulmate love, is it? Can pity be the bedrock of a beautiful love? Given Othello's inexperience of normal society, it seems like Desdemona's attentions are the first he's had to deal with. Both seem inexperienced in love: she falls for an exotic action-man, he falls for a starstruck fan.

Thankfully, Desdemona enters, but not before the duke belittles Brabantio's complaints with a deflating, 'I think this tale would win my daughter too'. A sense of impatience at this colourful but distracting love story is clearly setting in as he tells Brabantio to 'take up this mangled matter at the best' and move on - hint, hint: hurry the hell up! Desdemona's first speech is carefully balanced by Shakespeare to show her dual allegiances to both father and husband and it is sequenced in a classic good news first, bad news last structure. Placatingly, she addresses her 'noble father' and thanks him for her 'life and education'. She knows her 'duty' as a daughter but deftly yet swiftly pulls the rug out from under his feet. Daughter time is over and wife-time is beginning: 'but here's my husband'. It's a brutally efficient way of telling her father that she's a grown woman now, no longer his little girl. The staging options for this scene are myriad, but they nearly all feature Desdemona placed between the two men in her life and elevated above her father in some way. Unsurprisingly, she moves decisively towards Othello to show her new alliance. Brabantio's terse response, 'God be with you, I have done,' is the most begrudging marriage blessing in all of Shakespeare and captures perfectly his devastation and humiliation at being duped by his 'friend' and his daughter. We might be impressed by the fact that Desdemona is allowed to speak on her own behalf before the senate and by the duke's fair handling of the situation.

The duke's willingness to be done with this sideshow distraction is reflected, though, in his rhyming couplets, which force order on this unseemly, unwanted chaos. His message is self-serving: time to move on, Brabantio! 'To mourn a mischief that is past and gone is the next way to draw more mischief on'. Brabantio's response is also delivered in rhyming couplets and would suggest that he cannot accept this injustice lying down, as instructed, but eventually he surrenders and lets the war council 'proceed to th'affairs of state'. It is a mortal defeat for this proud man and one that he never recovers from. We learn in Act V that he dies broken-hearted. However, he's not done yet. The practicalities of war require Othello to sail to Cyprus immediately, interrupting their wedding night and consummation of the marriage [a sort of dark, running joke in the play]. Rather than the traditional separation of husbands and wives in wartime, Desdemona boldly asserts her conjugal rights, demanding that she go with her husband to Cyprus: this wedding night is happening, no matter what! To be fair this is encouraged by her father's refusal to house her till Othello returns ['I'll not have it so']. Nevertheless it signals Desdemona's determination and strength of character. Tragically, it is the worst decision of her young life. And to amplify the tragedy, Brabantio's last contribution to the play is to ominously warn his unwanted son-in-law to 'Look to her, Moor, if thou hast eyes to see: she has deceived her father, and may thee'. Again, the use of the rhyming couplet gives this an extra, echoing power, a clanging finality that rings true. It also picks up the motif of Othello being unable to see what's right in front of him.

Cue exeunt as we all go off to war. Or so we expect. Rather than the obvious grand exit, we are, however, returned to the malcontents, Iago and Roderigo. Othello's first use of his much-used epithet 'honest Iago' towards the end of the scene brings the play's villain back to mind and also reminds us of his adept duplicity. In case we missed it, Shakespeare spends the next 100 lines reinforcing and expanding what we already know: Iago hates Othello and Roderigo is his dupe. Roderigo and Iago's conversation presents a distorted echo of the preceding Othello - Brabantio dynamic. Where Othello was coolly controlled and Brabantio emotionally extreme, here Iago seems pragmatically grounded and Roderigo the unstable, similarly ludicrous, jilted male. Roderigo's melodramatic whinnying about the powerless of the rejected lover and the emptiness of his life contrasts markedly with Iago's philosophy of self-determination and seizing the day: while Roderigo 'will incontinently drown myself' Iago believes that "tis in ourselves that we are thus or thus. Our bodies are gardens, to the which our wills are gardeners'. In the words of the professional athlete: 'you make your own luck'. Here, Roderigo's noble courtly lover comes across as ridiculous, underscoring his general status as hapless, whereas Iago's modern pragmatism seems much more sensible, if pretty cynical and self-serving.

How does Iago continue to keep Roderigo in thrall? By telling him what he needs to hear: Desdemona's marriage is doomed to failure. Brabantio sees it as a monstrous mismatch and Iago can use that. Cynically, Iago suggests that Desdemona 'will find the error of her choice' once the flush of first sexual encounters cools. In other words, she'll come to her senses. Not only is Iago dismissive about Othello's age but he also signals his own lack of wealth by constantly imploring Roderigo to 'put money in thy purse'. If he is to make himself attractive to Desdemona, then Roderigo needs to be simply young, wealthy and in the right place at the right time. AND if Roderigo continues to give Iago access to 'my purse as if the strings were thine' Iago will ensure he *is* the right man, in the right place. Just so Roderigo, and we, the audience know, Iago declares 'I have told thee often, and I tell thee again and again, I hate the Moor'. He presents a fantasy of a unified assault on the newlyweds that will benefit them both, mutually.

The first of Iago's seven soliloquies ends the scene, introducing a dramatic irony that is unbearable at times, especially later in the play. Referring to his enthusiastic, naive accomplice as 'my fool' and 'a snipe' shows Iago's complete contempt for Roderigo and displays without any disguise his malice, especially when referring to his exploitation of love-fool Roderigo as 'for my sport and profit'. Profit is one thing, hard-headed and opportunistic. But sport is something much darker, sadistic and cruel. The problem is we cannot help but listen to him and can't really reason for clemency, well, without creating a scene and being escorted out of the theatre. Showcasing his excellent acting skills, Iago introduces further justification for his hatred of Othello. Characteristically, though, it seems that his suspicion that 'it is thought abroad that 'twixt my sheets he's done my office' is no more than supposition. It has no more proof than the vicious slanderings of Desdemona later in the play. Additionally, it is not clear whether his hatred stems from the fact that he has been cuckolded by a Moor or the fact that he seems to think this is common knowledge. The presentation of his relationship with his wife, Emilia, later in the play suggests he's not worried too much about her. Instead, it comes back to a type of bristling, jostling masculinity that animates much of the mayhem in the play and perhaps it is this, mere toxic rivalry, that fuels his vicious hatred of Othello.

Like every cartoon villain, Iago reveals what he'll do to destroy his enemy. Unlike most cartoon villains, he will actually achieve his goal. We are still very early in the play, but Shakespeare gives us VIP access into this brilliant but poisonous man's mind. He literally concocts his malicious scheme in front of us, laying out the various puzzle pieces before him then assembling them with impressive swiftness: Othello 'holds me well,'; 'Cassio's a proper [handsome] man,'; Othello 'thinks men honest that but seem to be so and will tenderly be led by th'nose as asses are'. His sudden declaration, 'I have't, it is engendered!' is an exciting and intense moment, and usually one accompanied on stage by dramatic lighting or sound design. Shakespeare's language of grotesque mutation and darkness ['hell and night must bring this monstrous birth to the world's light'], positions Iago as an antagonist to be feared, but because the playwright gives him so many soliloquies, this villain becomes frighteningly fascinating too. He appears as an avenging devil of some type, revelling in the destruction he is to wreak. The linguistic antithesis of darkness and light feeds into an ongoing motif of opposites that Shakespeare explores in the play: light and dark settings, skin colourings, moralities etc. Again, the use here of the rhyming couplet gives this dark prophecy a scary finality, as if to say "That's settled then," while the repetition of the stinging Ts give it a suitably menacing sonic quality.

And so to Act II, which tantalisingly promises epic naval battles, fortress sieges and a vicious little viper, waiting to strike.

Act II

It is usual in Shakespeare - and indeed in many works of fiction - for the first act of a drama to set out key details of plot, introduce characters, get them on stage, establish relationships and contextualise the 'who', 'how', 'where', 'what' and 'why' of the rising action. Act II of *Othello* is curious in this sense as it has a sense of re-starting, of presenting the characters with a situation that is new to all of them. Taking them out of Venice and their known environment Act II crash-lands them on an exotic shore, all in the same metaphorical boat.

This raises some important questions: how 'new' is this new start? This certainly isn't the 'happily ever after' that we might imagine at the end of Shakespeare's comedies, which often finish with a wedding: instead it's a new setting that carries with it all the old prejudices and pain of these characters' pasts. 'What happened next?', Act I asks: Act II provides the beginning of the answer. But, more importantly, how does Act II affect the characters' relationships, and what impact will these changes have upon the rest of the play? In beginning to answer this, we'll focus on the first scene of this act from Desdemona's perspective.

First, a brief overview of Act II: we open on the imperilled island of Cyprus,  where Montano and the gentlemen provide an update on the threat of the Turkish fleet, taking turns to provide fresh news of the storm that is, as we watch, both dispersing this threat and transporting Othello quickly towards the shore. Cassio enters, having been separated from Othello by the storm. Desdemona arrives and spars wittily with Iago on the nature of marriage and fidelity, until Othello arrives after her with his attendants.

Once they've gone, Iago is left alone with Roderigo. Iago goads him to imagine Desdemona kissing Othello, 'so near with their lips that their breaths embraced together'. This is the sweet, loving kind of 'breath', not the poisoned 'breath' that Iago will later use to manipulate Othello's thoughts. Iago convinces Roderigo that he should provoke Cassio, and this opportunity swiftly arises with Othello's portentous proclamation that after the removal of the threat of battle with the Turks, everyone

present should enjoy 'what sport and revels his addiction leads him'. Iago manages to get Cassio drunk. Montano and Cassio fight. Othello enters and strips Cassio of his title. The Act ends with Cassio humiliated, Iago triumphant in the successful execution of his plan.

Let's go back to the beginning. After the compressed waterways and dark streets of Venice, Act II opens with extraordinary bluster and pomp, the flowing water of the canals whipped up into a tempestuous storm that blows away the old and ushers in the new. The assorted company arrive on land to hear that this storm has destroyed the Turkish fleet of ships, 'so banged ... that their designment halts': Othello lands on Cyprus, therefore, not as the military hero of his imaginings, but as the recipient of a tremendous, if not slightly embarrassing, stroke of luck. He has been transferred from Venice to Cyprus with the smallest degree of military achievement possible, that of not being killed in the storm that has felled his enemy. This feels like a sidestep for him, a military would-be-hero without an enemy to fight, a reputation unsupported by the bombast of recent heroics. In the gap of dramatic time that marks his journey across the ocean, nothing much has actually... happened. An odd new beginning, then, for this happy couple - especially odd for a marriage founded on the stories Othello has told Desdemona about his magnificent military exploits, which we learn about in Act I. Act II therefore takes the myth of Othello as that great warrior and explores how he will cope in a very different reality.

In this sense, this Act feels a little deflated when it starts - a little like Shakespeare was experimenting with a second draft of the same play. Verdi notices this in his operatic version, *Otello*, in which he cuts the first act altogether and opens in the middle of the great storm. Out of the chaos of the storm - or, at least, the morally 'chaotic' events that have taken place in Venice - *should* come the order of military hierarchy and the harmony of happy marriage. Because of this, it's important that Othello and Desdemona leave together at the end of Act I but arrive separately when they come onto stage in Act II. Somewhere between the two countries, there has been a kind of symbolic rupturing of their relationship, suggesting from the outset that they will spend the rest of their time on Cyprus misunderstanding each others' realities.

Set in a different place with a different culture and different values, further away from the heart of 'civilised' Europe, Act II also disrupts the hierarchies of other relationships from Act I. In Venice, hierarchy was patriarchal and familial [i.e. Desdemona and her father] as well as based on military or aristocratic rank. However, Act II quickly establishes that even the great love between Othello and Desdemona now exists within a military setting - Desdemona is referred to as 'our great captain's captain'. There is a big difference between this grand description and the reality, since Desdemona arrives alone and in the company of Iago, who - as the audience knows - has already set out to work against her. She may be Othello's 'captain', but as a very young, inexperienced woman, an ingenue in fact, she's unprotected and out of her depth in Sc. 1, forced to ask multiple questions to understand Iago's perfectly-rhyming, sing-song riddling 'There's none so foul, and foolish thereunto, / But does foul pranks which fair and wise ones do'. Desdemona is used to operating within the ranks of high society. In Act II she is removed from the security of cosmopolitan Venice and relocated within a functional, professional, hyper-masculinised military environment which leaves her scrabbling to keep up with Iago's witty 'banter'.

Desdemona is not the only wife or mistress to be taken to Cyprus, but in Sc. 1, Shakespeare chooses to focus our attention on Iago and Desdemona's battle of linguistic wit, in which she - like Othello - is made a symbolic outsider through Iago's manipulation of language. Desdemona uses prose in speaking to Iago instead of verse [prose, for Shakespeare, often indicating familiarity, ignorance, a lower socio-economic status or lack of education], putting them out of step with each other and furthering the metaphorical distance between them. She poses frequent questions, which make her vulnerable to Iago and which offer him control of their dialogue - 'What miserable praise hast thou for her that's foul and foolish?' Iago exploits polished metre and rhyme: the perfect rhyming couplets of proud/loud, gay/may, nigh/fly and frail/tail draw our own attention to his linguistically masterful performance, underlining the comparative weakness of Desdemona, who can only ask questions and be led to her next one by Iago's clever answers. Iago makes no attempt to 'take on' Desdemona in his way in Act I, but here, alone and comparatively friendless, Desdemona is vulnerable.

Notice that Iago stops talking immediately when Othello's trumpets are sounded. Othello's reunion with Desdemona shows their close linguistic relationship, since they equally share a line of iambic pentameter in their greeting: 'O my fair warrior!', he exclaims and Desdemona responds with 'My dear Othello!' Just as Desdemona has been locked into verbal exchange with Iago, the play shifts its spotlight to the conversation between her and her husband, other characters melting away in the play's focus upon their shared language and the intimate kiss. Where she was an outsider in conversation with Iago, she is an insider here, discovering as part of her new start on this island that she is out of step with other characters, marooned with only one real connection of trust to her husband. The beginning of Act II therefore offers us a tantalising glimpse of their potential 'happily ever after'. Desdemona hopes that the 'heavens' should permit that 'our loves and comforts should increase / Even as our days do grow', and for that moment, we see happy newlyweds looking towards their future hopes. Yet, on stage, the wolves are circling in the background: Iago and Roderigo watch over this display of affection, one of the last between the couple that remains unsullied by Iago's manipulation.

There were several glimmers of hope that things will be getting better in Act

II: The threats of the Turkish fleet and of battle are over; the obviously symbolic storm has blown over; the lovers have survived this storm at sea and are now reunited on a Mediterranean island; a holiday mood prevails. However, any hope that the remote island of Cyprus might function like the 'greenworld' spaces of Shakespeare's comedies - as an escape from the problems of Venice and as a place of restoration and rejuvenation for the characters - is immediately undercut, not only by Iago's dark presence, but also by the presence of the malcontent Roderigo in the first scene in this bright new place. One storm may have blown over, but a far bigger one is already brewing.

Act III

Act III shifts our attention from Othello's public responsibilities as defender of Venice to his private ones as a husband. It opens with Cassio attempting to win back Othello's favour. Although Cassio entreats the Clown to send for Emilia, the Clown's word play, mirroring Cassio's use of 'honest friend' with 'I hear not your honest friend, I hear you', anticipates further deception, undermining Cassio's authority. The Clown, a repeated trope in Shakespearean tragedies, appears only in twice in the play, Act III Sc. 1 and Act III Sc. 4, serving as a structural turning point as Othello's jealousy escalates and his downfall begins, making the audience question which characters truly embody power, truth and honesty.

In fact, it is Iago, not Emilia, who comes to speak with Cassio. Their exchange is rich with dramatic irony. Iago promises to 'devise a mean to draw the Moor / Out of the way' and repeatedly demonstrates disrespect through his noun choice, the 'Moor', othering and depersonalising Othello, echoing the opening of Act I and his use, with Roderigo, of the impersonal pronoun 'him' and 'the Moor'. Shakespeare's language choices convey Iago's insinuations that Othello's behaviour is racially determined. While not engaging in similar talk, Cassio nevertheless normalises this treatment of Othello by describing Iago as 'kind and honest'. In a further irony, these adjectives remind the audience of Iago's disingenuity and the self-focused motivations that drive his machinations.

Once Emilia enters, her speech, the longest in Act III so far, hints at her inner resources of strength and intelligence, which Shakespeare shows to be overshadowed by society's systematic patriarchy. It is clear, with Iago's appearance on stage before, rather than with Emilia, of the inequality their relationship; Iago uses Emilia merely as another pawn for his manipulative game and shows her no love or affection. Nevertheless, the audience is reminded that Emilia, despite this disempowerment, is arguably the play's most insightful character, with her alliterative reference to 'wholesome wisdom' reflecting not only her clear explanation to Cassio of Othello's emotions but also anticipating her ability, by the end of the play, to offer the greatest 'wisdom' to Iago, Othello and Desdemona.

Despite being so short, scene 2 provides a powerful reminder of how much Othello trusts Iago. When he asks that 'These letters give, Iago, to the pilot', his use of Iago's name contrasts with Iago's own discriminatory use of 'Moor'. The letters are symbolic of how trusting Othello is – an honourable trait that the Machiavellian Iago exploits – but also as a symbol of communication and miscommunication. Letters, moreover, are careful constructs by a writer that are vulnerable to the interpretation of the reader, just as Othello is vulnerable to being misrepresented by Iago. Othello tells Iago that he will be 'walking on the works', which, whilst translating as walking on the city's outer fortifications, could be interpreted as a symbol of Othello's own positioning, balanced precariously on the outside of society and in danger of falling beyond the safe 'walls' of his own position of power, if he listens to Iago and lets jealousy override rationality.

The longest scene in Act III is Sc. 3. Desdemona hears Cassio's pleas before asking Othello to reinstate him as lieutenant and the audience sees Iago's devious plan to cast doubt in Othello's mind about Desdemona's fidelity. Desdemona's innocent promises to Cassio are laced with irony, as she vows to 'intermingle every thing [Othello] does / With Cassio's suit'. Such intermingling is, of course, what happens later as Othello envisions Cassio in his marriage bed, as well as representing Iago's meddling and the ease with which 'every thing' begins to fall apart. Iago makes short, passing comments – 'I like not that' and 'steal away so guilty-like' – sly insinuations to catch

Othello's interest. The tragic protagonist responds with short questions, 'What dost thou say?', 'Was not that Cassio parted from my wife?' and 'Who is't you mean?', a syntactic pattern that undermines Othello's position of authority and puts Iago in the ascendancy. This conversation is juxtaposed with Desdemona's return to stage, where the audience sees how her pleading for Cassio will be interpreted by Othello. Othello's final remarks after she leaves foreshadow the tragic fate of their relationship, with his use of the dismissive 'wretch' contrasting with his treatment of Desdemona at the start of the play and the personification of 'perdition' and 'chaos' indicative of increasing doubts, prophesising his own eventual fate, as his soul is captured by perdition and the chaos reaped by Iago.

Once Desdemona leaves, Iago's manipulative ways become the scene's focus. Short, staccato dialogue conveys Othello's increasing paranoia and the adjective 'honest' is continually bounced between them, as the audience witnesses again how cleverly dishonest Iago is and how Othello's tragic flaws – his jealousy and his internalisation of external prejudices – allow his judgements to be irreparably affected. Othello echoes Iago's exclamation, 'Think, my lord!', binding the characters together, suggesting that Othello now 'thinks' as Iago desires him to. Repeatedly Iago pretends to be holding back his true thoughts as a strategy to arouse Othello's suspicions. It is a strategy that works like magic: Othello wonders 'if there were some monster in [Iago's] thought / Too hideous to be shown'. This personification is another irony - the audience knows just how monstrous Iago's thoughts are, yet Othello's blind trust causes him to believe the 'hideous' actions to be those of Desdemona, rather than Iago himself. The image also reflects the 'monster'

 beginning to take shape and grow in Othello's own mind. Once again, Othello ironically describes Iago as 'full of love and honesty'. With breath-taking slyness Iago suggests that 'Men should be what they seem; / Or those that be not, would they might seem none!'. This reinforces the almost hyperbolic irony of this scene, with modern and contemporary audiences aware that Iago is not what he seems and the use of 'none' implying that Iago is not a man at all; he is a monster. The repetition of 'seem' throughout the play is closely associated with 'see',

highlighting Shakespeare's exploration of how absolute binary thinking [black and white, good and evil] is too crude a mental schema for understanding a world in which individuals are not always as they initially seem.

Iago continues to claim that it is not for Othello's 'good' to 'know (his) thoughts', drawing on the language of value to describe a 'good name' as an 'immediate jewel', leaving a person 'poor' without it. The use of concrete, materialistic comparisons – repeated in Iago's riddling 'Poor and content is rich' speech – is part of a pattern of commercial language he employs throughout the play, reflecting his lack of sentimentality and metaphorically questioning what should be valued in life. Iago 'steals' and 'robs' the lives of others and feels 'rich' only when he is succeeding in destroying Othello's love and position of military power. On the one hand, the use of such language suggests a world in which money and profit is replacing duty and honour, on the other, as the currency is men's souls, it encourages the audience to draw comparisons between Iago and the Devil and wonder whether he is an embodiment of evil or, perhaps, an embodiment of vices lurking within us all.

It is in Act III Sc. 3 that Iago advises Othello, famously, to 'beware, my lord, of jealousy; / It is the green-eyed monster which doth mock / The meat it feeds on'. Iago repeats the 'monster' imagery from earlier in the scene, heightening the dramatic irony as the audience knows that 'jealousy' is exactly what he wants Othello to feel. The metaphor of 'meat' echoes Iago's general, cynical reduction of the best of human behaviour, such as love, to lower instincts of appetite and consumption. The personification suggests how little control Othello now has; jealousy – like Iago – has the power to 'mock' him. The use of the imperative, 'beware', adds to the shift in power, with Iago positioning himself as an authority. Othello resolves to 'see before I doubt; when I doubt, prove'. Shakespeare expresses how the things that we 'see' are not always as they 'seem'. The irony is that Othello does not follow his own advice; he never sees Iago for what he really is, nor does he see Desdemona be unfaithful. Despite trying to convince himself to do 'Away with love or jealousy', it is his inability to deal with doubt that actually causes his
destruction of love.

Iago's poison acts fast and spreads quickly. Othello's soliloquy reveals how rapidly his feelings are infected and corrupted. Now claiming to 'loathe' Desdemona and the 'appetites' that he believes her to have, Othello echoes Iago's toxic attitudes towards both race and gender, drawing attention for the first time to himself as 'black' and lacking 'soft parts of conversation' and comparing Desdemona to a bird. Othello's comparison to a 'toad' anticipates his speech in Act IV, comparing Desdemona to 'a cistern of foul toads'. Invariably in Shakespeare's play toads are symbols of foulness and of loathsomeness and they are often associated with poison. Hence the choice of image suggests how, with help from Iago, Othello has swallowed society's worst prejudices. In this thinking, both he and Desdemona are like animals - him for being 'black' and Desdemona for being a woman. The tragedy is that now even Othello is thinking in this poisonous way. The imagery of the 'forked plague' refers to a cuckold, a 'monster' often depicted as a man with horns. Contextually, *Othello* was produced in 1603, a year with occasional outbreaks of plague. Hence, a contemporary audience may have felt the power of this extended metaphor and the irreversible, devastating consequences when a plague, literally and metaphorically, spirals out of control.

Desdemona appears briefly back on-stage. The significant time she has spent off-stage in this scene underlines her diminishing power, both societally and in marriage. After the handkerchief is dropped, Emilia picks it up and, knowing that her husband covets it,  gives him the 'thing'. We see Emilia's conflicting interests and, although she demands that he 'Give't [her] again', it is too late; her desire to please Iago leads to the betrayal of Desdemona. At this stage of the play the audience may wonder the extent to which Emilia colludes in her husband's plans. The handkerchief is the 'ocular proof' that Othello demands and his mirroring of Iago's theft imagery, describing 'He that is robb'd' and 'stolen', demonstrates Iago's malign influence and makes the audience question how similar Othello has become to the villain, now that he is overcome with 'waked wrath'. Once Iago reveals the 'bloody' handkerchief, Othello determines to 'furnish' a 'swift means of death / For the fair devil'. The juxtaposition of 'fair' and 'devil' conveys Othello's tormented emotions - Desdemona is still 'fair', despite Othello falsely believing her to be the 'devil'.

By Act III Sc. 4, Othello believes Desdemona has betrayed him. When he commands her to 'Give me your hand; this hand is moist', the imperative encapsulates his need to assert dominance and the adjective 'moist' conveys his assumption of her adultery. Rather than letting Desdemona speak for herself, Othello demands her to 'Lend me your handkerchief'. His claim that it was a charmed gift given to his mother and 'To lose't or give't away were such perdition' heightens the tension, with the repetition of 'perdition' from earlier in Act III foreshadowing their ill-fated futures. Unaware of Othello's hostility, Desdemona's demand to 'talk' of Cassio only makes matters worse, whilst Othello continues to demand to see 'the handkerchief'. Whereas In Act I Othello had been keen for Desdemona to be allowed to speak, this stubborn exchange underlines Othello's unwillingness now to listen to his wife. The final line, Iago's claim to be 'your own', mocks the language of marriage and conveys the power of his deceit to destroy their love.

Act III Sc. 4 concludes with a conversation between Cassio and Bianca, where Cassio's exploitation of his mistress is exposed. This is important because it shows that it is not just Iago or Roderigo who use women for their own ends; such behaviour is common among the men in the play, even the reputedly good ones. Emilia already knows as much and tells Desdemona so in the preceding scene. Here Emilia displays an experience and a wisdom in contrast to her mistress' naivety, informing a disbelieving Desdemona that men 'are all but stomachs, and we all but food' and that they 'belch us' when finished. Using the food metaphor, Emilia conveys her resentment at how men treat women as objects to satisfy their needs and, in doing so, becomes the increasingly assertive voice of truth – and, arguably, Shakespeare's mouthpiece – for how such inequalities persist. Emilia contemplates how 'jealous souls' are 'jealous for they are jealous: 'tis a monster'. The resonating 'monster' metaphor from Act III Sc.4, combined with the repetition of 'jealous', emphasises her insight at how jealousy can overwhelm love and logic, thus foreshadowing the tragic deaths caused by Othello's blind jealousy and Iago's manipulative scheming.

Act IV

The plot is now afoot and Iago's plans gather increasing pace. If he can just dupe Othello into believing Cassio is talking about Desdemona and not Bianca, then the Moor's mind will slip decisively into revenge. As we have noted, at times the action of the play verges close to comedy, opening up the possibility of the avoidance of a tragic ending. The duping scene in Act IV, Sc. 1 recalls scenes from *Much Ado About Nothing* and *Twelfth Night*, where characters are similarly tricked into false beliefs. In *Othello*, however, the potential for comedy only makes the tragedy sharper and more bitter. We must remember too that during this scene Iago continues to play a very dangerous game. If he over or misplays his hand, his machinations will be exposed and his life forfeited.

The Act opens *in media res*, which means in the middle of action. Iago's opening question is a response to something already said, as if we have joined the pair mid-conversation. In some ways, nothing has changed. Iago and Othello are once again engaged in intense discussion of Desdemona's alleged infidelity. On the other hand, things have changed a little since we last heard them conspiring together in Act III, Sc. 4. At the end of that scene where they kneel together and swear a sort of allegiance, Othello's mind appeared to be decided, his intentions resolute and his course determined: 'O, damn her, damn her!... I will withdraw / To furnish me with some swift means of death / For the fair devil'. In the interim, it seems Othello has, however, had further doubts, as here he is questioning Iago closely for more concrete evidence of his wife's unfaithfulness.

Of course, as ever, Iago leads his master on a merry dance, expertly twisting the knife of his torture, now making Othello picture Desdemona in bed with Cassio. Pretending to be holding back what he knows to protect Othello, he whets his master's increasingly feverish appetite, an appetite to know the very worst most salacious details, making him wait, making him tease out the dire implications for himself. It's like a form of water torture. Iago raises the possibility, for instance, that Cassio may have confessed, but only when

---

Othello eagerly swallows this bait, does Iago fully reveal that Cassio has already told him that he has had sexual intercourse with Desdemona. It is a lie, of course, and a perilous one.

While the audience, or any witness to this scene, might pause and wonder why Iago didn't just spit out what he claims to know, rather than prolonging the agony in this drip-drip-feeding manner, Othello's imagination is so overwhelmed by what he has been made to picture that the 'Othello music' disintegrates into a series of single words and bewildered questions and exclamations: 'Pish! Noses, ear, and lips. Is't possible? Confess – handkerchief! O Devil!' and he falls into a fit. With poison coursing through his mind and now also through his body, Othello is in no condition to reflect on what he's just been told or to speculate about Iago's motives.

How should the actor playing Iago perform this scene? Is Iago a sadist, enjoying tormenting his master? Does he seem all concern and sincerity to Othello during this conversation, but then take any opportunities that arise to smile and wink at the audience, almost in anticipation of their applause for his cruel brilliance? Like a matador finishing off a bull, does he deliver his final blows with a flourish? Or is it a sour Iago who stands over the prostrate figure of his master and says 'work on / My medicine, work!', a bitter man grimly intent on getting his revenge? Whatever way Iago is played, he only has a moment to relish his work before he has to put his mask back on as Cassio arrives on the scene.

Naturally, Iago takes this opportunity to further poison Othello's reputation. While his master is unable to hear him or defend himself, he tells Cassio that he should not disturb Othello's fit, for doing so may lead him to breaking out into 'savage madness'. When Othello recovers, he seems, momentarily, to pick up the insincere tone of Iago's patronising 'Have you not hurt your head?', responding with 'Does thou mock me?' As elsewhere in the play, for just a moment, he is agonisingly close to discovering Iago's villainy and the whole tragedy being averted. But Iago's scornful admonishments to 'be a man' and the thought of Cassio having intercourse with his wife sweep away this thought. Othello has no time to think, as Iago instructs him to hide and hear Cassio speak of 'where, how, how oft, how long ago, and when/He hath, and is again to cope your wife'.

While Othello does as he is told and hides, Iago once again has the stage to himself. And once again, he takes the audience into his plans, as if inviting our admiration. In the exchange that follows, Iago shows he is just as adept at manipulating Cassio as he has just been with Othello.

Though he may have disgraced himself by drunkenly fighting with Montano, Cassio is considered to be an honourable, courtly character, a gentleman. Up until the fight, he was liked and trusted by Othello and he is despised by Iago in part because of his fine courtly manners. To her face, he is respectful and affectionate to his mistress, Bianca, repeatedly calling her 'sweet Bianca'. However, now, behind her back, in the locker-room banter with Iago, Cassio expresses vile, misogynistic attitudes, scornfully laughing at Bianca's affection for him and describing her belittlingly as a 'fitchew' – a smelly polecat. The insulting language he uses in this scene about Bianca contrasts starkly with the courtly terms he had used previously to praise Desdemona – a lady so exquisite that she 'excels the quirks of blazoning pens'. As at the end of Act III, we are again reminded here that misogyny in the play is not the preserve of Iago or Roderigo and of how, in this patriarchal culture, women were often worshipped as saintly virgins or despised as whores.

Of course, Iago's ruse works a treat, with Cassio's scorn only salting Othello's wounds. Once again, it seems like Iago might be enjoying himself, exacting a sort of revenge on Cassio. By saying 'I am a very villain else' it is almost as if he is showing off, flaunting his villainy in front of their faces, rubbing Othello and Cassio's noses in it, like an actor or matador playing to the gallery. Cassio is oblivious to the clue and is even assured at the end of the scene that Iago is looking out for his best interests.

Now, after what he has just heard, surely Othello will be putty in Iago's hands. Except that, even at this stage, there is a seesawing in Othello's mind as he tries to reconcile his hatred for Desdemona's supposed infidelity with his enduring love for her. Each time he expresses hatred and the desire to punish her 'let her rot and perish'; 'she shall not live'; 'hang her' it is counterbalanced and overpowered by feelings of tenderness and love – 'A fine woman, a fair woman, a sweet woman'; 'O the world hath not a sweeter creature'; 'O she will sing the savageness out of a bear'. Iago is alarmed, as his urgent interjections signal: 'Nay, you must forget that'; 'Nay, that's not your way'. For, despite all of Iago's efforts, Othello's mind could still tilt in his wife's favour. Until, that is, Iago has the brilliant notion to flip Desdemona's qualities against her; 'She's the worse for all this'. Having horrified Othello with the thought of Desdemona's deceit and falseness, Iago then makes him feel responsible for allowing his wife to continue to sin. Finally, Iago has him entirely. Enraged, Othello imagines meeting out justice in the form of savage violence: 'I will chop her to messes'.

But the tragedy is still not yet inevitable. The arrival of the authority figure of Lodovico in Cyprus might just put a spanner in Iago's works, bring the world back into better balance and, as Desdemona says, 'make all well'. We can imagine how Iago might say the lines 'I am very glad to see you, signor' through gritted teeth. Immediately Lodovico asks after Cassio and letters from Venice inform us he is to be made governor of the island. Then Lodovico witnesses Othello strike Desdemona. Shocked, he asks for an explanation for Othello's behaviour. Who does he ask? Honest Iago, of course. As ever seizing the cards that fall into his hand, Iago confirms that Othello is 'much changed' and, using a signature tactic, pretends he is reluctant to reveal what he knows while also almost revealing his duplicity: 'It is not honesty in me to speak / What I have seen and known'. Lodovico is the third nobleman Iago has deceived and manipulated in just one scene. He's a villain but, we have to admit, he is very good at it.

Starting scene 2 in a similar way, mid-conversation, with Othello seeking more evidence of his wife's affair, conveys the backwards/forwards circularity of Othello's thoughts. It is the same pattern we saw between the kneeling scene in Act III and the start of Act IV and in the seesawing, antithetical ways he describes his wife to Iago. Tragically, Othello does not give any credence to what Emilia says, dismissing her avowals of her mistresses' faithfulness because she is just a 'simple bawd'. Then Desdemona enters. Here is another chance for the play to take a different, happier turn. If Othello could ask her directly whether she has had an affair with Cassio, she would have a chance to deny it. He could mention the handkerchief and she could tell him how she dropped it. But he doesn't ever ask her directly about Cassio or the handkerchief, talking instead in general terms and utterly confounding her. All she can do is swear she is honest and all this does is make her seem more dishonest in his blinded eyes.

In the ensuing conversation about Othello's treatment of his wife, Desdemona seeks comfort from Emilia and from Iago. Iago plays his innocent role with ease, until his wife gets uncomfortably close to the truth: 'I will be hanged if some eternal villain / Some busy and insinuating rogue…/ Have not designed this slander'. This is dangerous talk and he needs to move quickly to close it down, 'Fie, there is no such man; it is impossible'. Emilia, however, is not so easily going to be diverted. In fact she is intent on shining a spotlight on a

potential villain: 'The Moor's abused by some most villainous knave / Some base notorious knave, some scurvy knave…' Iago's tense, curt comments try to shut her up before anyone puts two and two together. Perhaps he squirms a little, a bead of sweat perhaps breaking out on his forehead. It's almost like a pantomime, tempting the audience to shout out, 'He's behind you!'. In a further irony, Desdemona saves Iago from potential exposure, by asking him, at length, to go and speak to Othello on her behalf.

As Emilia and Desdemona leave, Roderigo enters. Again, so close. If either woman had come back into the scene or overheard the two men talking, everything would have been different. But they don't and it won't be. In a short space of time, in a succession of two-handers, we see how brilliantly Iago keeps all his malign plates from crashing down around him, as he confers first with Othello, then Cassio, then Lodovico, then Desdemona and Emilia and now Roderigo.

Each of these encounters has presented danger for Iago. Now he finds Roderigo is also going to be a problem. Roderigo accuses Iago of not dealing 'justly' with him and complains that all the 'jewels' he has given to Iago to give to Desdemona, despite Iago's assurances to the contrary, have had no effect at all on her affections. Indeed, belatedly, Roderigo suspects that he might be being 'fopped'. Hence, he will speak to Desdemona directly, make her return his jewels and cease wooing her. He is determined to do so and presumably she must be close by, as she only left a minute or so ago. It is an indication of Iago's cleverness or Roderigo's stupidity that the former is swiftly able to convince the latter to desist in this sensible course of action and instead engage in a plot to murder Cassio so that, somewhat improbably, this will bring him closer to winning Desdemona.

Act IV closes with the only prolonged women-only scene in which Desdemona's unworldly innocence comes against Emilia's worldly wisdom. As this encounter is considered at length in other sections of this guide, it is not necessary to go into it in detail here. Many critics have worried about the characterisation of Desdemona from hereon in. In particular, her passivity, her willingness to accept her fate and her unwillingness to blame her husband are hard to equate with the courageous young woman who went against her wishes and the racist codes of her society to marry Othello. During the willow song, Desdemona pauses after singing 'let nobody blame him; his scorn I approve', realising that 'that's not next'. As so often happens in the play, momentarily a space opens up in which other outcomes become possible. Here Desdemona reflects that she doesn't have to passively accept her doom. As with other such fleeting moments in the play, however, they are soon gone as the play drives relentlessly to its inevitable tragic denouement.

Act V

Like Act I, Act V begins with Iago and Roderigo plotting night-time mischief on the streets. In fact, the night-time setting settles the yin-yang struggle between darkness and light in the play's various settings. The play starts in darkness and ends with darkness, tipping the play world into the black, literally, symbolically, emotionally and morally. The dramatic pressure of the plot has been building to almost unbearable levels and we feel that it surely must erupt into mayhem. In Act IV, Othello's odious treatment of his wife, Iago's crowing manipulation and the promises of murder and vengeance all combine in a heady brew that must be drunk, liked or not. It is compelling theatre for sure and Shakespeare's breathless plotting hurtles us through humiliation and hubris and swiftly onto horror. Only Cordelia's murder in *King Lear* rivals Desdemona's brutal end in its heartrending pathos. Both women are made exemplars of female purity and goodness by Shakespeare, thus maximising the horror and tragedy of their grisly ends.

Shakespeare provides a notable foil between worldly and pragmatic Emilia and innocent and idealistic Desdemona in the last scene of Act IV. Whereas Emilia sees adultery as a forgivable fault ['The world's a huge thing: it is a great price for a small vice'] Desdemona's almost prudish retort, 'Beshrew me, If I would do such a wrong for the whole world!', firmly positions her as the ideal wife, the angel at home. Along with Shakespeare's none-too-subtle moral message, Emilia's rant that 'I do think it is their husbands' faults if wives do fall,' encourages the audience to identify fully with the innocent victim, rather than the tragically duped killer. Even more affecting is Desdemona's naive hope that laying the wedding sheets on their bed may remind Othello of the luminous love that began the play. The fact that she genuinely seems to believe that 'my love doth so approve him that even his stubbornness, his checks, his frowns [...] have grace and favour' transforms her into an emblem of goodness, with a capital G, rendering her almost more symbolic that realistic, despite Othello's frankly despicable behaviour towards her [publicly assaulting her, privately berating her, and in some productions roughing her up behind closed doors]. Her brightness is what makes Othello and Iago's

---

darkness more impenetrable.

The fact that the opposition of Good and Evil can be couched numerically like this points to the overwhelming power of Evil in the play world. It's two against one, violent men against gentle woman, and this doubling up, like Roderigo and Iago plotting against Cassio, reinforces the play's dark horror. We can feel what's coming and dread its arrival. Appalled but also fascinated, we cannot look away. With Emilia's stinging rebukes of husbands ringing in our ears, it's also clear, just in case we've been distracted, where our sympathies should lie. Shakespeare doesn't even need to do this - the character dynamics so powerfully guide our sympathies that surely we must not even consider sympathy for Othello until *after* he kills Desdemona. That said, on the other hand, depending on our religious convictions, his concern for the fate of her soul might generate some sympathy for him, perhaps.

But rather surprisingly, Act V doesn't deliver the unimaginable. Rather the play nimbly skips into part two of the 2-for-1 murder offer made in Act IV. Cassio's time has also come. But this is only the appetiser before the main course. In a way, despite Cassio's innocence and strengths as a character, he is no longer of consequence to the audience, mere collateral damage in a dirty war. Dramatically, what it allows Shakespeare to do is to prolong the inevitable, leaving it festering and mutating in our minds while we get caught up in the murky mayhem and action of Act V Sc. 1. It also allows Shakespeare to completely solidify Iago's status as villain, shifting from immoral to amoral. His attacks on innocence and his cynical exploitation of others is nothing new, but the callousness of his remark that 'now, whether he kill Cassio or Cassio him, or each do kill the other, every way makes my gain' marks the darkest depths his virtuosic opportunism has reached to date. While the necessity to eventually get rid of Roderigo - The Man Who Knows Too Much - Iago's assertion about Cassio is puzzling. On par with his conviction that Othello has cuckolded him, his belief that Cassio 'hath a daily beauty in his life that makes [Iago] ugly' suggests a self-contempt and paranoia that is unusual in such an accomplished and confident villain. But how seriously can we take the words of such a truth-twister, really?

Regardless, we're here for the dastardly action not the meaningful motivations. Cue dirty street fight where characteristically '*Iago from behind wounds Cassio in the leg*'. Iago's acting performance in the mayhem that follows is masterly, again echoed in his performance in Act I Sc. 2 where he declares 'You Roderigo! Come sir, I am for you'. But here his acting is amplified to deadly intent. His stabbing of his foolish accomplice is treachery of the highest kind, but it does occasion the first deliberate outing of his true character. Unlike Emilia's ironic complaints against the 'base notorious knave' who has slandered her mistress in Act IV, Roderigo's dying yelps of 'O damned Iago! O inhuman dog!' come closest to exposing Iago's true nature to the characters around him. It is a moment of high tension for Iago and the audience, less so for the unsuspecting characters around Iago on stage. The highwire balancing act that Iago conducts in this scene, as he does elsewhere, is reflected in the brevity of his aside, where we'd probably expect a soliloquy, at the end of the scene. Only a line and a bit, his observation that 'this is the night that either makes me or fordoes me quite' reflects the unstable conditions swirling round him as he tries to control them as best he can. He knows he's in danger, but more importantly for the audience, Desdemona is now in mortal danger.

While Act V Sc. 1 has mostly been about Iago and his unending skulduggery, Othello plays a brief but terrifying cameo that prepares us for Sc. 2, in no uncertain terms. As he hears his former friend and trusted ally, 'good Michael,' scream for help, bleeding in the street, he coldly listens to his agony while thanking 'O brave Iago, honest and just' for teaching him the ways of 'justice'. Another disturbing moment, made more appalling by the mad violence of Othello's language. His declaration of 'strumpet, I come' is so different in its brutal brevity to the lyrical beauty of his earlier lovestruck language that it is jarring and alarming. The heavy assonance and aggressive Ts of the rhyming 'blotted' and 'spotted' promise a barrage of actual heavy violence, while the repetition of 'lust' carries a frightening duality of meaning: Desdemona's imagined lustful appetites, but also Othello's very real and frightening lust for her 'blood.'

The sudden lurch from noise-filled outside to quiet inside, from dark street to dark bedchamber, is a dramatic change and Othello's swift entrance on stage 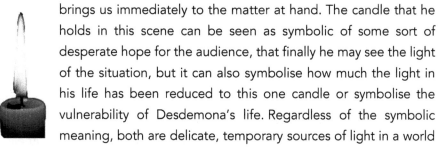 brings us immediately to the matter at hand. The candle that he holds in this scene can be seen as symbolic of some sort of desperate hope for the audience, that finally he may see the light of the situation, but it can also symbolise how much the light in his life has been reduced to this one candle or symbolise the vulnerability of Desdemona's life. Regardless of the symbolic meaning, both are delicate, temporary sources of light in a world full of darkness. It's not a good sign, especially given Othello's blindness to the startlingly obvious. The change to the private world should also remind us of the promised vengeance he feels must be exacted, one suggested by Iago of course, with Othello dutifully 'led by th' nose as asses are'. Iago's urging in Act IV Sc.1 to 'do it not with poison, strangle her in her bed - even the bed she hath contaminated' is what the audience prepares itself for, making Desdemona's idea to 'lay on my bed my wedding sheets' a futile act of appeasement. The person she is trying to appease is no longer the man she married. And so we watch with great trepidation this madman, or maddened man, creep into the calm, pure, tender space of their bedroom. The awful moment has arrived. There is no pause or fast forward button on the performance. Endure it with Desdemona we must and the awfulness of the situation means that endurance, in the most literal sense of the word, is required. This is undoubtedly one of the most difficult scenes to watch in all of Shakespeare's plays.

Having Othello justify his actions to himself, essentially externalising his warped conscience to the better-informed audience, then having Othello demand that Desdemona atones for her 'sins' has two primary effects on the audience. Firstly, it maximises the agony, taking 83 suspense-filled lines from Othello's stage entrance to his despicable murder. Secondly, it allows us to become enraged at his wrongheaded vengeance and gullibility. The fact that he waits until this moment to confront his wife with his lethal suspicions when no one else can intervene makes it such an uncomfortable audience experience. Most productions amplify the injustice of this moment by using physically intimidating actors to play Othello, while choosing petite, delicate actors to play Desdemona. For example, in The Bristol Tobacco Factory's excellent 2017 production of the play, Othello was played by Abraham Popoola, a formidable 6ft 5in presence who bellowed like a bull when angry, whereas Desdemona was played by petite, 5ft 5in, Nora Lopez Holden with a giddy schoolgirl energy. This physical contrast was extremely effective when it came to this scene above all others.

However, the enormity of what Othello is about to do confronts him at the very start of this scene. Theory is not the same as practice. While Othello is clearly an experienced soldier and must have killed his fair share of men before this story begins, deciding to kill his wife is an entirely different matter. Mere days ago, he had declared that 'when I love thee not chaos is come again'. This time, however, chaos does not come to Othello. Othello brings the chaos all by himself. Repetition of the distancing phrase 'it is the cause' three times shows us how hard he tries to convince himself to carry out his grisly plan and how he shies away from responsibility. Furthermore, the violence and degraded animalistic imagery of his language since coming under Iago's spell has disappeared temporarily. In fact, he returns to the lyrical beauty of some of his earliest speeches. The beautiful descriptions of her skin as 'whiter than snow [...] and monumental alabaster,' the 'light' and Promethean heat' that she had brought to his life and the 'O balmy breath,

that dost almost persuade Justice to break her sword' are all elegantly sensual and almost trick the audience into thinking he will change his mind, if he could just stop and think more clearly. Even his contemplation of the irreversibility of his 'justice' is beautiful in its rose metaphor: 'when I have plucked the rose I cannot give it vital growth again, it needs must wither'. Like the paralysing trance of enraged jealousy he suffers in Act IV, he seems to fall into another trance as he inhales the potential of what might have been, a blissful alternative universe. Again, repetition underscores the difficulty he has in undertaking what he promised. He repeats 'one more' three times, inhaling the sweetness of Desdemona's being like it is a drug. Smelling his sleeping wife is weird, granted, but his kissing her breaks the spell, like a grotesque version of Snow White or Sleeping Beauty. Instead of waking up to her dream husband, Desdemona will wake up to a nightmare. Lying prostate on the bed, she is entirely vulnerable and dreadfully unaware of what we, the audience, are witnessing. And the minute she wakes her fate is sealed.

While the dream version Othello gazes at seems to neutralise his wrath, the real wife in front of him hardens his heart and his resolve. The harshness of his language returns, fuelled by his rather dubious logic that 'she must die, else she'll betray more men' - how selfless of him, putting others before himself! The subsequent exchange between the estranged pair is swift [through frequent use of stichomythia], fractured and literal, rinsing the beautiful imagery from Othello's mouth. His primary concerns are about whether she has 'prayed tonight' and he  urges her to 'confess thee freely of thy sin'. He seems willing to condemn her body to death but not her soul to hell. But, thankfully, Desdemona, who in some productions can be dangerously passive, at least protests her innocence and denies the charges, so much so that Othello protests that she 'dost stone my heart and makes me call what I intend to do a murder, which I thought a sacrifice!' This momentary wavering in Othello's resolution is ruined by Desdemona's characteristic but very foolish weeping for the injured Cassio. Common sense would urge her to placate the deranged husband that confronts her rather than provoking him: 'Out strumpet, weep'st thou for him to my face?' But for this poor woman 'it is too late.'

His smothering, or in some productions the choking/strangling, of her is horrific. As we have said, it is a deeply disturbing experience for the helpless audience, who knows he destroys his most precious possession mistakenly but cannot help feel an intimacy to such horror, akin to a group of executioners. Shakespeare further intensifies the moment by having Desdemona cry out 'O Lord! Lord! Lord' as she dies, which is immediately echoed by Emilia's interrupting 'My lord, my lord! What ho, my lord, my lord!' Shakespeare denies us even a moment to process what has just happened and instead ramps up the tension. It is an unsettling linguistic echoing, described by Granville-Barker as a 'macabre duet'. So now destructive external forces have encircled one character and move onto another, our sort-of-protagonist, Othello. Fate has found his wife and now it's about to find him. Like she had no time to escape, now he finds he's out of time too. Othello's frantic confusion is all too obvious in the extremely fractured speech Shakespeare gives him from lines 89 to 99: it is full of caesuras, sentences fragments and emotionally all over the place as he veers from trying to cover up what he's done to *realising* what he's done: 'What wife? I have no wife!' So disordered are Othello's thoughts that he feels his mental chaos precedes a type of apocalyptic cosmic mayhem: 'methinks it should be now a huge eclipse of sun and moon and that th'affrighted globe should yawn at alteration'. In other words, he's going to be found out and his world is gonna come crashing down around him.

Not only is he about to be unveiled as the opposite of the noble, 'valiant Othello' that graced the start of the play but his plans, literally, don't go to plan. 'Murder's out of tune' as Cassio has not been killed and to make matters dramatically worse, Desdemona revives, long enough to truly rattle Othello but also long enough for her to cement her angelic status in the play. She doesn't reveal all, tabloid-style, but instead, when Emilia asks who has done this to her, protects Othello's reputation: 'Nobody. I myself'. Othello's declaration that 'you heard her say herself it was not I,' when she says nothing of the sort, is the mother of all Freudian slips and could only come from a frenzied mind, buckling under huge stresses. The fact that he has the perfect get-out clause, a misleading confession from his victim, should be ideal. Instead, he completely bungles it by confessing and then justifying his actions: 'Twas I killed her. [...] She turned to folly and was a whore'. His crude language carries frightening echoes of Iago: 'Cassio did top her: ask thy husband else'. This mention of 'thy husband' brings Iago back into the consciousness of the audience but also echoes Emilia's complaints about husbands at the end of Act IV. In total, the word 'husband' is repeated 10 times, which almost borders on the comical, but captures the disbelief of Othello and Emilia at the situation they find themselves in, whilst also portraying a slow clarity forming. This laboured focussing of the characters slows down *the* moment of revelation [in Aristotelian terms the play's anagnorisis], the one that will spell the end for Iago. It is the last time that the audience carries the burden of the lashings of dramatic irony Shakespeare has heaved onto our shoulders. At last, our emotional exhaustion begins to ease. Sort of.

Emilia's narrative role shifts from obedient wife and ignorant accomplice to social moraliser. She shouts the truth for all to hear, connecting the dots in a way that Othello simply could not, blinded as he was by the 'green-eyed monster,' jealousy. She is the first to expose Othello as a 'gull,' a 'dolt, as ignorant as dirt!' Whereas previously she played the role of obedient wife, supplying Iago with Desdemona's misplaced handkerchief, here she becomes the disobedient wife, declaring: 'I will not charm my tongue, I am bound to speak: my mistress here lies murdered in her bed'. Through her repetition of the words 'villain' and 'villainy', Emilia also proclaims to the other characters that foul play is afoot. These words are repeated no less than 11 times in this scene, conveying the pervasiveness of evil in the playworld. Her insistence that "Twill out, 'twill out!' unravels the threads of Iago's web of intrigue. The longer people talk, the more vulnerable he becomes and he does what any decent villain would do: he tries to silence the source, who just happens to be his own wife. He tries twice, succeeds once, then scarpers. Emilia dies a symbol, not of wifely obedience to her husband, but a symbol of sisterly solidarity, requesting to be laid 'by my mistress' side'. That she dies poignantly singing the willow song Desdemona sang in Act IV Sc. 3 further unites the two women as victims of a vicious patriarchy. While the wives mirror each other in their song singing, the husbands are united in their uxoricide [fancy term for killing your wife].

The tension of the scene has escalated steadily once Emilia begins to chirp and encourages others to see with their brains as well as their eyes. Othello's devastating anagnorisis finally comes at line 195. Such is the damage done to his sense of self that it can only be articulated through noise - no words will do only a prolonged roar of anguish: 'O! O! O!' Like King Lear's inexpressible grief in *King Lear* at his daughter's death ['Howl, howl, howl,

---

91

howl, howl'], Othello's pain is beyond language itself, rendering words tragically inadequate. Like all the great tragic heroes, his pain is a crushing mixture of regret, outrage, despair and shame. Of all the tragic heroes, though, Othello must surely be the most pathetic and humiliated. He is the only one who directly kills that dearest to him.

All tragedies end with some restoration of order, the banishment of chaos and optimistically some sort of social recalibration. These restorations of order are not always convincing; see *Macbeth* and *Hamlet*. The idea of justice being done and good finally regaining its rightful place in the cosmic order of things  are reliable indicators of whether meaningful change will come. While Othello certainly adheres to the Aristotelian concept of the tragic hero in his huge fall from grace, by the play's end no social lessons seem to have been learned; the Venetian elite closes ranks and chalks this off to an unfortunate calamity resulting from the actions of a few oddballs. Othello is a Moorish outsider; Iago an unusually evil malcontent; root these out and all will be well. The play can be read as a warning about embracing outsiders and otherness in general: best to stick with what we know. Justice is ultimately, albeit unsatisfactorily, done. Othello condemns himself to hell by killing himself while Iago is captured and will suffer for his malice. Case closed.

Maybe. Iago is indeed captured but he is frighteningly unrepentant, defiant even in his brazenness. When Othello demands a reason for the carnage Iago has deliberately unleashed, he cannot address him directly, such is his disgust: 'demand that demi-devil why he hath thus ensnared my soul and body?' The obvious retort to that is that Iago didn't ensnare Othello's body and soul, he did it himself. What Iago does is even more threatening: he refuses to give any reason or motivation at all: 'Demand me nothing. What you know, you know. From this time forth I never will speak word'. Cooperative and compliant he isn't. This refusal to justify his actions is frightening in several ways. Firstly, it points to the unnerving, compelling power he wields, even in defeat. Secondly, not only does it point to the deep-grained malice of Iago's mind but it also makes his actions terrifyingly random. Evil is just something that happens to decent people and there's not much we can do about it. The fact that such evil festers within Venetian society itself, rather than being smuggled into the society by a much more easily identified black outsider can only bring discomfort, rather than reassurance. Lodovico's closing remarks that the deathbed containing Desdemona and Othello, and in some productions, Emilia, 'poisons sight, let it be hid' points to a hushing up that is typical of the play. Dangerous, unpleasant things hide beneath a veneer of sophisticated society. It is only a matter of time before such darkness erupts back to the surface. Control and order, then, seems only to be a temporary state of affairs.

Not that optimistic then in terms of society learning lessons, then, or satisfying justice being enacted on the villain. What about the growth in self-awareness of the protagonist? Surely Othello learns something about his ordeal? Again, maybe. While Othello resigns himself to an afterlife of suffering for his grievous errors, which is satisfying for the audience in some way, his final speech engages in some swift damage control to his reputation [why would he care at this stage?] or displays the type of fatal short-sightedness that fuelled the entire disaster to begin with. His speech to Lodovico and Gratiano demands truth ['speak of me as I am. Nothing extenuate, nor set down aught in malice'], which is fair enough given Iago's gross distortions of the truth. However, he claims himself to be 'one that loved not wisely but too well, of one not easily jealous, but, being wrought, perplexed in the extreme'. Not many audiences can swallow that type of self-delusion without acute nausea. How exactly can he convince himself that he 'loved [...] too well?' And too well for whom: himself or Desdemona? It is an odd statement to make but one that smacks of telling his story to 'extenuate'. It is also worrying in that it sounds like the rubbish a dominating partner in an abusive relationship would spout. Rightly he points out to his 'being wrought', but his actions were not proportionate to the alleged 'crime' committed. Even the striking metaphorical beauty of comparing himself to 'the base Indian [who] threw away a pearl away richer than all his tribe' or his transition to a man overcome

---

by emotions who 'drops tears as fast as the Arabian trees their medicinable gum' fails to distract from the blame that lies at his door. He may be trying to distance himself from his own actions or trying to deceive himself, but it's not a convincing performance. In fact, Othello is indulging in exactly the type of truth-twisting that Iago is so good at and that is worrying in itself, as if Othello has been permanently warped by prolonged proximity to Iago.

So, at the end we have the prerequisite Shakespearean Tragedy high body count: Othello dead, Desdemona dead, Emilia dead, Brabantio dead, Roderigo dead, Iago presumably soon dead. Also, order is restored and a new world order established, in that it's doubtful any more Moors will be allowed to enjoy status in Venice. At least Cassio is now governor of Cyprus, but the old order remains in Venice with the duke presumably still leader of the city state. The new social order is going to be a very white one. Justice has sort of been done and lessons have sort of been learned and a sort of evasive regret uttered. The future looks sort of the same as the present? *Othello* is not a play that promises great cathartic change and this is mainly due to the fact that evil remains so strong and goodness so vulnerable.

The soliloquies

What makes us who we are? What we say about ourselves or what we do? How we treat others? What we think and feel? Is the quintessence of identity external and revealed through our social interactions, or is it internal and revealed by what's really going on inside our heads, hearts and, if we believe in them, our souls?

What's the function of a soliloquy? This dramatic device is the equivalent of extended interior monologue used in novels; it takes us right into the intimate private thoughts of a character. Creating an empathetic link between audience and the character who soliloquises, the dramatic device also helps shape where our sympathies lie. Crucially, by convention, in Elizabethan theatre characters tell the truth in soliloquies. However untrustworthy and duplicitous the world around them, however much they need to put on masks and pretences in public, in their soliloquies characters drop these masks and speak honestly. Of course, Shakespeare is particularly adept at showing us how characters change and adapt themselves in different contexts. Often the public self is itself a kind of performance, a playing of a role, or, in Iago's case, multiple roles. Think, for instance, of how he shapeshifts, adapting the way he speaks and behaves to play the roles of villain, loyal servant, husband, friend, confidante and so forth.

In Shakespeare's plays, the public self is often a mask or façade and contrasts starkly with a hidden self that is only expressed during private interactions with a trusted partner, friend, lover or spouse. Iago, of course, is a master of masks, but he lacks anyone in the play with whom he can converse honestly. Compare him, for instance, to Hamlet who has his reliable friend Horatio by his side for most of the play, or King Lear who has his wise fool, the dutiful Kent and, in the end, his daughter Cordelia. In contrast, despite being married and having a wife who could potentially be a confidante, Iago is very much alone. Hamlet and Lear are also the tragic heroes of their tragedies. In those plays the villains – Claudius and Edmund

– are only allocated one soliloquy each, because it is the hero's story that we are following. Tellingly, of course, in *Othello*, Shakespeare reverses this pattern, with Iago having far more soliloquies than his master.

As Simon Palfrey puts it in *Doing Shakespeare*, Iago is 'at once bluffly reliable and impregnably dishonest'. Palfrey suggests we might look for insights into Iago's real self in these soliloquies. Except that, bucking their conventional revelatory function, even his soliloquies are 'less than transparent'. Although they can be played in different ways by different actors, fundamentally, watching Hamlet's soliloquies, we feel that we are witnessing the unfolding of his deepest, most private thoughts. In contrast, Iago's much shorter soliloquies seem more like speeches, addressed to the audience, as if he is talking to us as much as to himself. Whereas Hamlet's soliloquies take us into to his mental state -  viz his tortured, circular thoughts as he wrestles with his revenge task - in Iago's soliloquies he calmly takes us into his malevolent planning, almost as if we are sounding-boards for his thinking and even his co-conspirators. Knowing that he fools everyone else and leads them by the nose, the audience is suspicious too that the same process is taking place in soliloquies that only superficially seem transparent.

The comparison with Hamlet is also helpful, in that, in some ways Iago can also be seen as an avenger. Like Hamlet he is plotting private revenge against a leader who comes to embody state justice. Unlike Hamlet, however, although he has to improvise as he goes along, he does not waiver or hesitate in his action, yet we never really discover what he hopes to achieve. Hamlet seeks to kill Claudius in order to avenge his father's death. What does Iago hope to achieve by his actions? What would be his perfect outcome? Certainly, even in his soliloquies he does not tell us and perhaps he doesn't know.

As many critics have noted, the effect of Iago's soliloquies is two-fold. Firstly, they make the audience queasily complicit in his machinations. And though we might be morally appalled by his plans, we are likely to be intrigued to see whether and how he pulls them off. We might even admire his ingenuity, as he seems to want us to. His plans drive the drama and make it compelling. He is also charismatic, in his own dark way, and, in some ways a sardonic comic, ridiculing human follies. Hence we can feel uncomfortably close to Iago. Secondly, as they take us closer to Iago, his soliloquies push us away from the other characters. Due to the dramatic irony of knowing what they do not, we might even consider the other principal characters to be somewhat foolish and credulous, so easily manipulated as they are by clever Iago.

Notoriously, in his soliloquies Iago offers several possible explanations for his motives. Critics generally agree that none of these – revenge for not being promoted, revenge for Othello sleeping with Emilia, simple hatred of Othello and so forth - seems sufficient in themselves to explain such destructive hatred and determined, merciless wrongdoing. Nor are they convinced that combined they provide enough explanation. Famously, Samuel Taylor Coleridge suggested that Iago is, in fact, seeking to explain his actions to himself in his soliloquies, and Coleridge's memorable description of this as the 'motive-hunting of motiveless malignity' is well-known and often cited. Of course, not all critics agree.

By leaving uncertainty about his real, true motivation, particularly in comparison with the much simpler motivation supplied by the source material, Shakespeare makes Iago into an enduring enigma. His soliloquies reveal he is an astute reader of human nature and that he is capable of recognising, even admiring the noble qualities of his adversaries. His estimation of the character strengths of Othello, Cassio and Desdemona and of what makes them vulnerable to manipulation is always precise and telling. Similarly, he quickly appreciates the lack of these qualities in Roderigo. In some ways, he operates almost like a chorus in Greek tragedy, stepping out of the action to comment on it. Unlike a chorus, however, he is also like the dramatist orchestrating each scene and making other

---

characters do as he wishes. Combined, these elements make him a highly complex and elusive character, as we will discuss further in our section on him later in this guide.

And what of Othello? Where are his soliloquies? Hamlet is given seven. Iago has five, albeit briefer and more focused ones. Like the villains in *Hamlet* and *King Lear*, Othello is only allowed one soliloquy and that comes right at the end of the play in its final scene. In comparison, Iago's soliloquies begin in Act I and are dotted regularly through the subsequent action. By the time we are given access to Othello's thoughts it is thus too late for us to feel the same sort of connection with him as we have with Hamlet or, indeed, with Iago.

In Hamlet's soliloquies he asks profound questions, most famously about the nature of death and what might happen after death. Big questions. Questions that express new, humanist doubts about inherited religious teaching. In comparison, Othello's soliloquy is less philosophical. Shakespeare could have had his hero here thinking about the nature of justice or the tormenting passions of love. Instead, he presents Othello as much more focused and concentrated on the task at hand and still struggling to reconcile his love for Desdemona with his hatred for her crime and his role as judge and jury. As we have seen before, Othello is struck by how innocent and beautiful his wife looks as she lies helplessly sleeping. Her skin is pure, 'whiter' than 'snow', and unblemished, as 'smooth as monumental alabaster' and he thinks of her as a 'light' he has to extinguish. She is also a 'rose', a conventional symbol of female beauty. Even her breath is sweet: 'O balmy breath'. As they have ever since Iago started to poison his mind, these tender observations and the feelings of love they elicit in Othello struggle against his conviction that he must kill her for her crimes or else she will 'betray more men'. The dramatic effect is excruciating because he is so agonisingly close to recognising the truth, and has been for such a long time, that Desdemona is indeed as he describes her, not just in her appearance, but in her pure, unblemished nature.

Critical essays on characters

There are dangers in providing exemplar essays. Inadvertently, such exemplars can close down the space for your own thinking and encourage uncritical regurgitation of an essay's content in examinations. Our essays were not written in timed examination conditions and they are not examples of what an examination board would expect from any student in those conditions. Hence, primarily, our essays are not designed as model answers. Moreover, fundamentally we don't believe there can be one model answer to literary questions. Instead, we contend that the best essays express pupils' own critical thinking and opinions, aided by their teachers and informed by engagement with other readers. Hence our aim in the following essays is to provoke, stimulate and inform your own thinking about the play's major characters and make you reflect more critically on their roles and functions.

Hopefully, our essays will make you think again, perhaps even make you think differently. Sometimes you may also encounter readings with which you disagree. Good; so long as you can explain and justify why you have come to different conclusions. Indeed, often at A-level it is more useful to cite those with whom you disagree as this encourages you to engage with the criticism. You may also find our writers offer slightly different shades of interpretations in these essays. Again, good, particularly if you can evaluate these differences and decide where your own opinions lie. Whether you mostly agree with the interpretations or not, these essays should, however, provide plenty of information you can digest, ponder, alter, reformulate and contest in your own words.

Remember when you are writing about characters to try to lift your perspective above the character-level action of who said what and who did what to the author-level perspective of why these words and actions are significant.

Othello

1

'Othello is surely the stupidest of Shakespeare's tragic heroes. Discuss'. Okay, 'stupid' is probably too cruel and crude a term to apply to this unusual Shakespearean tragic hero, although it was used by the famous critic, F.R. Leavis. Unlike Hamlet, Lear and Macbeth, Othello is an outsider – a mitigating factor undoubtedly - but if we read his character in Aristotelian terms, his specific hamartia or character flaw is one of the hardest to forgive. Whereas Hamlet's procrastination may be forgiven due to his grieving father-worship and Lear's pompous pride tempered by his senility, like Macbeth's ruthless ambition, Othello's gullible jealousy is harder to accept. The first Afro-American actor to win an Oscar, Sidney Poitier, refused to play Othello, claiming that 'I cannot go on stage and give audiences a black man who is a dupe'. Now, while this points clearly to the racial aspect of Othello's character it also spotlights his foolish gullibility. Certainly, Othello's jealousy and gullibility are infuriating and hard to forgive when Shakespeare makes us watch him destroy the life of a completely innocent young woman.

So, why is it so important to measure Othello's, let's call it, naivety, rather than stupidity? The audience needs the wriggle-room in which we can garner some sort of sympathy for him. If we cannot do so, we will condemn him as stupid. If we can sympathise with him, however, we will feel the pain of what it's like to be fooled by a wilier foe. Iago relishes Othello's [and everyone else's] suffering and the cruelty with which he torments Othello is despicable. Othello's torment is one that can only be pitied and through this pity

Shakespeare opens an avenue to forgiveness. The shame and humiliation that Othello feels at the play's end happens to us all, so it is a very recognisable, intimate pain. If we know this pain, or at least can understand it, we can forgive him, or at least try to, rather than judge from afar and condemn him outright.

Luckily, Shakespeare allows us the potential to forgive because as Othello complains in Act V, he was 'being wrought, perplexed in the extreme' by a cruel and masterful manipulator. While it's virtually impossible to forgive his murder of Desdemona, we can at least understand what drove him to such desperate violence, despite the despicable consequences. All tragic heroes suffer greatly and Othello is no different. His fall from respected general to pitied and despised outcast, from happy husband to maddened murderer involves tremendous emotional suffering and the fact that it happens in such a compressed time frame, basically three nights, results in a tragedy of immense, claustrophobic power. His fall is so swift, his transformation so sudden that if the audience did not see it happen before their very eyes it would seem nigh on ridiculous. You cannot just hear this story, you have to watch it. What must be agonising for Othello, compared to the other notable tragic heroes, is that his life journey moves from lowly slave to 'valiant' commander and then to self-damned soul. Unlike the other tragic heroes, born into the higher echelons of their societies, Othello's ascent was as steep as his descent. But like all these men, he is in some way responsible for his own downfall.

While it is undeniable that Iago pours pestilence in Othello's ear, firstly against his dear friend Cassio, and secondly, his beloved wife, Iago is not technically responsible for Desdemona's death. Ultimately, Othello extinguishes her life, not Iago. Othello commits the murder and legally would not have a leg to stand on.

2

Othello's impulsive and ferocious anger is more shocking because of his calm authority at the start of the play. Despite the cruel racist jibes of Brabantio in Act I and the threat of arrest, Othello responds with admirable restraint and steadiness. Later, alerted to Cassio's drunken brawling in Act II, Othello's treatment of his friend is unbiased, clear-sighted and business-like. Even later in Act III, it seems he has wisely let the drunken brawl blow over and intends to reinstate Cassio at an opportune time. Let's not forget also how the Venetian senate praised and esteemed his military prowess; he is 'valiant' and 'noble' and shows great respect to his social superiors. Additionally, as critics such as Wilson Knight have noted, Othello's language is lyrically eloquent and respectful, especially in his account of his courtship of Desdemona. Nevertheless, his many positive attributes are not enough to save him. They do, however, make his descent into violent jealousy much more dramatic.

It seems that, professionally, all these positives allow Othello to thrive but when they are transplanted into domestic civilian life they are of no use, becoming hindrances instead. The unexpected, almost light-switch change in his character is carefully prepared by Shakespeare, though, but this only becomes apparent with hindsight, in study rather than in performance. Not only is Othello trying to adjust to civilian life in sophisticated Venice ['rude am I in my speech / And little blest with the soft phrase of peace'] but he is clearly out of his depth when it comes to the intricacies of romantic relationships. Shakespeare creates a mismatched marriage that seems like romantic bliss to the lovers but aberrant and even unnatural to everyone else. Othello is, crucially, aware of their differences, noting in Act III's pivot point that 'haply for I am black / And have not those soft parts of conversation / That chamberers have, or for I am declined / Into the vale of years'. Although rarely ever played as such on the modern stage, Desdemona is not much more than a child, whereas Othello is middle-aged, so the age gap is substantial and problematic. [Naturally, Iago plays this very card repeatedly.] His wife has fallen in love with him through his stories of heroic deeds and their love is an old-fashioned, idealised type of courtly love, completely out of kilter with the world around them. Their marriage is between a girl who wants to experience life's exciting potential and a man who has already done so and wants to settle to the stability of domestic bliss. Additionally, Othello's ignorance of sophisticated society is too easily manipulated by Iago's talk of 'supersubtle Venetians' and their 'pranks'. Essentially, the marriage is a union of two ingenues: Desdemona's sheltered inexperience of the world is mirrored by

Othello's unworldly ignorance of cultivated Venice. Under pressure, a relationship that seemed securely based on pure, romantic love begins to crack. Arguably, Iago just accelerates an inevitable process.

The fault lines may have always been there but covered over by the control that Othello could wield in a warrior's world, a world in which orders are to be obeyed and actions have clear consequences. There is also something a little too subservient about Othello at times, maybe a little too grateful to his Venetian superiors for his high status, as if his 'service' is a commodity that buys his respect. Unfortunately, for such an exotic but ultimately useful outsider, he never realises that once his usefulness expires so too will his status. Othello's self-belief and trust is destroyed all-too easily by Iago because Iago removes Othello from the very place where he can cover up his inadequacies. Othello's self-destruction ignites in Act III Sc 3, and it doesn't take much in all honesty. While he reasonably demands 'proof' of Desdemona's betrayal, it takes very little persuasion to convince him that 'she's gone!' That Iago does not need to do much to engineer this U-turn is frightening; rather than employ the self-restraint that characterises him to date, Othello flings himself in completely the opposite direction. Given that Othello has spent most of his life in the hypermasculine world of soldiers and battles, it is, perhaps, no surprise that he goes to pieces when considering what Graham Bradshaw describes as 'one of Shakespeare's recurrent and even obsessive nightmares: the nightmare of double betrayal, in which a character thinks [...] that the man he loves most has stolen the woman he loves most.'

The transition from sure-footed warrior to bewildered husband is summed up memorably by A.D. Nutall, who describes the play 'as the story of a hero who went into a house [and] became a kind of nothing'. Controlling his wife and fending off male rivals is the duty of a good husband. Moreover, as Sean McEvoy points out in Shakespeare the Basics, a warrior's core identity rested on the steadfast love of a true woman. And, if his wife is unfaithful, the warrior becomes a monster, a cuckold. Failure to control his wife would not only undermine Othello's authority and his sense of self, it would turn him into a despised cuckold. While his paranoia about being cuckolded is striking, Iago's suggestion that it could be his close friend who has cuckolded him is devastating. It destabilises Othello's world so completely that the Othello of Act I and Act II is barely recognisable compared to the Othello of Acts III, IV and V. His confident self-control is replaced by a wild instability and thirst for violence that is appalling to watch. Even his language, formerly measured and elegant, becomes frenzied and fractured, see particularly the speech that precedes his fit in Act IV Sc 1 or his promise to 'chop her into messes'. The paranoid, vindictive husband he becomes, one forged in a furnace of jealousy and insecurity, is ultimately punished by Shakespeare for these very qualities, posing a clear moral message for the audience. Mistrust and suspicion destroy marriages and the people in them. The fact that both genders are punished is particularly notable, but the blame, as voiced by Emilia in Act IV, lies with the husbands not the wives.

3

Pamela Mason observes that Othello is just one of several jealous men in Shakespeare's plays, standing shame-faced with characters such as Leontes in *The Winter's Tale* and Posthumus in *Cymbeline*. All their suspicions are shown to be completely misplaced and all are humiliated and punished appropriately to atone for their unreasonable behaviour. This focus on the private world of relationships relegates the political saga of Turkish invasion to mere background and the concentration on human relationships, rather than political forces, makes the play's focus shockingly familiar. The irreversible poisoning of personal relationships is all too universal, as an anonymous critic noted: 'Love and jealousy are passions which all men, with few exceptions, have at some time felt; the imitation of them, therefore, finds an immediate sympathy in every mind'. The fact that both protagonist and antagonist come from the homosocial environment of a renaissance army, an environment that only sees women as sexual conquests or strumpets and brothels as places of 'love', may explain the distorted views of women in the play. Ultimately, the men of the play reveal an almost inevitably degraded view of romantic relations with women: even the suave, refined Cassio treats Bianca, a courtesan, with contempt. F.R. Leavis goes as far as to accuse Othello of being 'egotistic', interpreting his winning of Desdemona, who should be completely unobtainable, as a huge ego-boost for him, a type of refutation of social assumptions about his supposed inferiority. Essentially, Leavis is unconvinced there is any real love between the two. Decrying Othello's 'ferocious stupidity', Leavis claims that Othello really, only loves himself and that Desdemona is merely an object that makes him feel better about himself. Harsh!

The unspoken assumption behind Leavis' claims is in marrying Desdemona that Othello is doing well *for a beastly Moor*. Othello's racial status is an essential part of his character, both in terms of how he sees himself and also how others see him. There is an entire stage history of white actors in blackface playing Othello and a subsequent reclaiming and rejection of the role by black actors. Hugh Quarshie argues that 'when a black actor plays a role written for a white actor in black make-up and for a predominantly white audience, does he not encourage the white way, or rather the wrong way, of looking at black men, namely that black men [...] are over-emotional, excitable and unstable'. Some critics see Shakespeare's portrayal of Othello as a radical recentring of a  traditional outsider by making him the protagonist and engineering sympathy, however limited that may be, in a predominantly white audience. Whatever way it is seen, Othello's racial character is complicated and complicates the play. Even the racial composition of the audience can affect audience responses in strikingly different ways.

A bone of contention often gnawed upon is whether the play itself, or even Shakespeare himself, is racist. The play is too slippery for simplistic 'yes/no' answers. Undoubtedly, the abusive language used to denigrate Othello is racist and it attacks Othello's visual difference relentlessly. Brabantio, Roderigo and Iago are undoubtedly and unashamedly racist in their beliefs and words. For a Jacobean audience, the colour of Othello's skin carried connotations of evil and corruption, blackening Desdemona's good name.

Dehumanising language used to describe Othello perpetuates racist stereotypes of Moors as primitive, sexual predators and symbols of Muslim barbarity and threat. But Shakespeare tries to defuse these hostile stereotypes in a number of ways.

Firstly, Othello is a Christian convert, not a Muslim, as proven by his constant talk of heaven, hell, sin, souls and damnation. Karen Newman suggests that 'by making the black Othello a hero, and by making Desdemona's love for Othello, and her transgression of her society's norms for women in choosing him, sympathetic' Shakespeare challenged the dominant racist norms of his time. Certainly, Othello's high social status would have been surprising for a culture that saw Moors predominantly as slaves or refugees of Spanish oppression rather than skilled military leaders and trusted generals. The nobility and sophistication of his thoughts on love and the general lyrical beauty of his language, initially at any rate, is far away from racist stereotypes of primitive savagery. At the start of the play, certainly up until just after he dismisses Cassio, Othello is a principled protagonist, espousing the importance of love, courage, responsibility and loyalty and giving his new wife licence to speak for herself. However, the problem is that this nobility does not last long.

4

Anna Thompson described Tommaso Salvini's famously tempestuous Othello performances as showing that the 'Moor has only a veneer of civilisation which Iago effectively peels off, thereby exposing the barbarian within'. Whatever we think of Thompson's description, the emergence of Othello's uncontrollable emotions and his bellowing for bloodthirsty vengeance seem to reinforce rather than undermine such racist stereotypes. Nigerian writer Ben Okri sees *Othello* as depressingly limited in its positive portrayals of blackness, describing the protagonist as 'the white man's myth of the black man'. Certainly, it is true that Othello does not seem to trigger any introspection about how Moors should be treated differently in society nor does he seem to have a high enough social status to fundamentally challenge the racist philosophies of characters like Iago and Brabantio. In one way, Othello's portrayal in the play still renders him a type of slave, a slave to

Venetian politics, a useful tool that can be cast aside once his usefulness has spent itself in 'service,' as he puts it. In reality, Othello's racial isolation is not made the centre of the play at all. Rather there is a more universal warning about jealousy and impulsiveness, human failings not exclusive to Moors or people of any creed, culture or race. Certainly, Othello's race cannot be ignored, but it is not essential to his tragedy: he could have been white and still have endured essentially the same journey, but it may not have been as lonely.

Although many critics have expressed and promulgated racist readings of the character of Othello, as early as 1694, Charles Gildon expressed a more enlightened view in his rebuttal of Thomas Rymer. Arguing that Othello's jealous violence is not prompted by his race, Gildon wrote that unless Rhymer 'can prove that the colour of a man alters his species and turns him into a beast or a devil, 'tis a vulgar error to allow nothing of humanity to any but our own acquaintance of the fairer hue'.

5

Blackfacing was common until the mid-twentieth century and it remained illegal for a black man to play Othello on the stage well into the twentieth century. In the modern world of colourblind casting, can *Othello* still work? Maybe. Notable experiments have been conducted, one of the most striking being the RSC's 2015 production where both Othello and Iago were played by black actors. This casting complicated Iago's racism profoundly, turning one black man against another and denying the brotherhood one might, perhaps naively, hope for. Rather than Iago being an insider and Othello an outsider in Venetian society, they were both outsiders: when Iago says he knows '*our* country disposition well', in this production, he is referring to a national identity he shares with Othello, somewhere where women's behaviour can be trusted. This choice of casting made Iago's racism more monstrous, more cruel and his ambition more ruthless.

The RSC production also made the two men more alike than different, bringing to the surface something that is disturbing to contemplate. Is Othello Iago's shadow brother? Or is it the other way round? While much is made of

Othello's visual blackness, Iago is really the black hole which creates the shocking vortex into which the playworld is pulled, distorted and destroyed. His moral blackness annihilates all with which it comes into contact. Iago's actions are as much driven by jealousy as Othello's as Catherine Bates observes Othello's miraculous eloquence finds its demonic counterpart in Iago.

Othello is an unusual play in that the antagonist speaks more lines than the protagonist [Othello speaks 860 lines, Iago 1097]. Shakespeare gives Iago seven soliloquies compared to Othello's three. There is a deep, complicated connection between the two men, one that is disturbing, murky and threatening. From a Freudian perspective, the battle between Othello and Iago could even be read as a dramatisation of the conflict between the id and the ego in our minds: Othello represents the ego and its need to restrain the primal desires of the id. Othello's striving to control his emotions contrasts with Iago's stoking of those very emotions. When Othello's self-restraint disintegrates in a conflagration of jealousy, his personality becomes frighteningly unstable. Othello becomes the very thing he tried so hard not to be. His lurching from zero to hero and back to zero with no self-control, from idealised love to hateful murder and back to regretful love warns the audience that we know not what we are capable of. But the play is even more disturbing still: Othello *becomes* Iago in the frenzy of his rage. He becomes cruel, vindictive, cynical, paranoid and even begins to sound like his nemesis, portraying romance as mere hyperfertility, a 'cistern' of lust and degradation, a quagmire of betrayal and exploitation. As F.R. Leaves puts it 'Iago's power […] is that he represents something that is already in Othello: the essential traitor is within the gates'. All Iago had to do was teach Othello to be himself, to let his 'real' self out. The outcome of this battle, and its ominous warning about the ugly truths that hide within all of us, helps create the crushingly pessimistic tone of the play's end.

Desdemona

Desdemona, the tragic heroine in *Othello*, embodies the key themes of injustice and inequality. Despite her initial positioning as a woman with agency, actively seeking the love and life that she desires, over the course of the play, she becomes a victim of Iago's manipulation, as her own husband, blinded by jealousy, murders her for a crime of which that the audience – and, finally, the tragic protagonist – know her to be innocent.

In the play's opening scene, Desdemona does not appear on stage but is introduced through the dismissive language of male characters: Iago, her father Brabantio and the antagonist, Roderigo. Desdemona has no control of Iago's inflammatory depiction of her in the act of sexual intercourse, as he describes to Brabantio how 'his daughter and the Moor / Are now making the beast with two backs'. This graphic, animalistic imagery reflects how society's dominant misogyny easily misconstrues women; she is immediately judged by her supposed sexuality rather than her true character. Brabantio laments the 'unhappy girl' who has married 'the Moor. That infantilising 'girl', coupled with his claim that she 'deceives me', where the verb 'deceives' misconstrues her actions, expresses Brabantio's certainty that he should have full control over his daughter. Brabantio continues to dismiss Desdemona, questioning 'How got she out?', as if she were an animal to be locked up and tamed. Rather than celebrating her love, Brabantio wishes to 'apprehend' her and Othello, like criminals. Throughout the whole first scene her name is not used once; she is sexually objectified, demeaned, misjudged and viewed as a possession.

Othello, in contrast, uses Desdemona's name in Act I Sc.2 to assert his 'love' for 'gentle Desdemona'. Desdemona finally appears on stage herself in Act I Sc. 3. Though she is able to tell her own story, the fact that she needs permission to do so emphasises women's subordinate positionality in a society strongly governed by patriarchal norms and values. Brabantio demands that state business be put on hold now that he has discovered his daughter to be 'charmed' by Othello and orders his men to 'Fetch Desdemona hither', an imperative that continues to treat her dismissively. Desdemona respectfully addresses her father, contrasting with the previous characterisations made by Iago and Brabantio, as she asserts her own position, as 'hitherto your daughter'. Although she only speaks twice in this scene, she demonstrates her true love and agency, with 'downright violence and storm of fortunes' conveying it is her choice that she 'lives' with Othello and must, she insists, travel with him to Cyprus despite the dangers.

Repeatedly Shakespeare introduces Desdemona through the lenses of male characters. In Act II, Cassio describes Desdemona as 'divine' and 'our great captain's captain', the use of this military title signalling her perceived power over Othello. Ironically, it is Iago – who Desdemona travels with – who becomes the real 'captain' of Othello as the play develops and the one with power to 'fire' his 'spirits'. Initially, however, Desdemona is the recipient of Othello's love and respect.

As well as the courage and independence of mind Desdemona has shown in making her marriage and standing up to her father, she also demonstrates wit, playing along with Iago's dismissal of Emilia and all women, suggesting that she does 'beguile / The thing I am, by seeming otherwise'. This witty word play indicates Desdemona's confidence and intelligence, although it could also be interpreted as a boldness that gives Iago fuel later to persuade Othello that what he 'sees' in Desdemona is not all what it 'seems'. When Desdemona questions how Iago defines a 'deserving woman', he concludes that even the most ideal woman should limit herself to 'suckle fools and chronicle small beer'. This degradation of women reminds the audience of the atmosphere in which Desdemona must hold her own; despite her ability to match Iago and tease him, calling his final argument 'lame and impotent' and question if he is 'not a most profane and liberal counsellor?', her gender causes her to be seen as inferior.

When Othello enters the stage in Act II Sc. I, Desdemona's love for him is clear. Delighted to see her 'dear Othello', Desdemona claims that 'our loves and comforts should increase,/Even as our days do grow!'. The metaphor of growth captures her love, yet this is juxtaposed with Iago's subsequent scheming plan to seize the fact that 'Cassio loves her' for his revenge plot. The audience sees Desdemona occupying contradictory positions: she is both an articulate, demonstrative woman, invited to speak for herself in front of the Senate, subverting a contemporary audience's gender expectations, but she is also an oblivious pawn in Iago's game. Critics, such as F. R. Leavis, unimpressed with how easily Othello is hoodwinked by Iago, tend to

underplay Desdemona's courage and intelligence. It's significant that she too is taken in by Iago's loyal façade, as this confirms it is a convincing disguise.

Desdemona's final appearance in Act II is brief. She asks only 'What's the matter?' about the commotion following the fight and Cassio's dismissal, as orchestrated by Iago. At this point in the play, the audience can see the tensions between masculine violence [and military honour] and true love, as Othello reassures his 'gentle love' that this is 'the soldiers' life'. Desdemona remains central to the conversation between Iago and Cassio, and Shakespeare hints at how Iago will take advantage of her 'gentle' character, planning to 'turn her virtue into pitch'. Thus her innocence is juxtaposed with his villainy and her final tragic fate, and her lack of agency in preventing it, is foreshadowed.

Desdemona's next appearance, in Act III Sc. 3, shows how her righteousness is used as a weapon against her. Repeatedly she reassures Cassio, 'Do not doubt' before entreating Othello to reinstate him, 'as I should entreat you wear your gloves,/Or feed on nourishing dishes, or keep you warm'. This is her first lengthy onstage conversation with her husband and displays her independence and kindness. Whilst the triple of comforting comparisons conveys Desdemona's sense of justice, the imagery of 'feed' also foreshadows the imagery of consumption used later when Othello recognises that jealousy, 'the green-eyed monster', 'feeds' on 'meat', signalling how Desdemona's care for Cassio feeds Othello's jealousy and his doubts about Desdemona's fidelity.

The dropped handkerchief in Act III Sc. 3 marks a turning point for Desdemona. Desdemona reassures herself that 'my noble Moor / Is true of mind and made of no such baseness / As jealous creatures are', which is ironic, since the audience has just witnessed his 'jealous' nature. Their dialogue becomes short, fragmented sentences, reflecting the increasing tension as Othello's obsession with 'the handkerchief' overrides love and reason. Desdemona's earlier self-confidence is eroded, evident in her conversation with Emilia, when her use of military imagery 'unhandsome warrior' reflects her self-doubt and uncertainty as to why Othello has started a 'war' with her.

Desdemona's 'handkerchief' continues to dominate Act IV when Othello and Iago enter the stage mid-conversation. In contrast to his earlier praise of 'gentle Desdemona', Othello does not mention her name now, focusing on his reputation and his belief that 'A horned man's a monster and a beast'. His fear of being made a cuckold reveals how his masculine identity is based on the control of his wife and her sexual behaviour – losing control of her, he loses his sense of self. Despite Desdemona showing only virtuous traits and a rejection of Venetian custom to pursue true love with him rather than another suitor, Othello is determined by this point to 'let her rot, and perish, and be damned'. This triple reveals the cruel, revenge-obsessed person that Othello has become, the verbs suggesting the violence and death that awaits Desdemona. Othello repeatedly describes her upcoming fate, threatening horribly to 'chop her into messes'. Desdemona is dehumanised by Othello's language, yet he also laments her as 'A fine woman! a fair woman! a sweet woman!' showing how jealousy and love battle for ascendancy in his thoughts. Although Desdemona is off stage throughout this dialogue, it is an insight into the contrast between her true nature and how she is misrepresented by her husband, so easily deceived by Iago.

Desdemona has become one of the principal puppets for Iago's scheming, particularly when Othello is convinced by Iago to 'strangle her in her bed', the bed that Othello falsely believes Desdemona to have committed adultery in. Desdemona reports to Lodovico and Iago that an 'unkind breach' has fallen between Othello and Cassio; though she is not yet aware, the audience can see the dramatic irony that the real breach is between herself and her husband. Continuing to plead for Cassio, wishing to 'atone them, for the love (she) bear(s) to Cassio', only fuels the 'fire' that Othello feels, causing Desdemona to question three times 'My lord?' before he strikes her, and calling her a 'Devil'. Once  again, ironically, the language Othello uses to degrade Desdemona is the language that applies to Iago. When Desdemona does not retaliate, maintaining her calm dignity despite Othello's behaviour, Othello repeats Lodovico's description of her as 'obedient', echoing the word mockingly to convey his contempt.

Whilst she demonstrates the strength of character to go against societal expectations, it could be interpreted that Desdemona's tragic flaw is her decision to interfere with Othello's public business, exacerbated by her continual imploring on Cassio's behalf. Shakespeare, therefore, could be seen to either be condemning the gender inequalities and acceptance of male violence against women or, from a less generous perspective, his characterisation of Desdemona could be interpreted as a warning about what happens when individuals challenge the values and norms of their society.

By Act IV Sc. 4, Desdemona has become powerless to convince Othello of her innocence. She stands by her honesty, reflecting that, though 'his unkindness may defeat my life' it will 'never taint my love'. The metaphor of war suggests that Desdemona has accepted her 'defeat', a contrast to her strength at the start of the play in justifying their love, the verb 'taint' reminding the audience of her unwavering dedication to Othello but also the 'tainting' of the marriage vows that she has been falsely accused of. Act IV reveals Desdemona's love as well as her ignorance about Othello's true intentions. Thinking he has ordered her to bed to reconcile, she sings the Willow song, a song about a sorrowful woman who feels so deeply for her lover that she accepts his hatred. 'All a green willow must be a garland./ Let nobody blame him, his scorn I approve', she sings. The reference to 'green' recalls the 'green-eyed monster', highlighting Desdemona's innocence and sorrow in comparison to Othello's raging envy. Her decision to not 'blame' him is followed by her 'good night', the caesura suggesting that, beneath her optimism, she knows their love is finished. This encapsulates the two sides of Desdemona, her despondence and heartbreak as well as her deeper insight, choosing a song in which the man – like Othello – falsely accuses his wife and banishes her.

By Act V, the audience knows that Desdemona's tragic fate is sealed. Once Othello enters the bedroom, Desdemona's repeated short questions, 'Who's there? Othello?... what do you mean by that?... Talk you of killing?' reflect her diminishing influence. Desdemona's final line reminds us that she is 'guiltless' and 'falsely murdered', before she forgives Othello, blaming 'Nobody, but myself'. This reinforces Desdemona's unwavering loyalty; despite Othello's actions, she is dedicated to loving him unconditionally. After Othello chooses to 'stifle' her, metaphorically highlighting his inability to listen or value her when so overcome by insecurity and envy, it is Emilia who informs him that he 'kill'd the sweetest innocent', demonstrating the strength of her character before she, too, loses her life for her loyalty. Her choice to sing Desdemona's Willow song shows the strength of female friendship and Desdemona's influence over her. The audience can interpret Desdemona's final line and this ending as submission, but also determination to stand by her decision to love Othello and to ensure that her moral goodness and kindness is not tainted by the actions of others.

While some critics view Desdemona as a weak and insubstantial character, in part because of her apparent passive acceptance of her victimhood, others are more impressed and sympathetic. A.C. Bradley, for instance, considered it an 'extraordinary and splendid thing' for a 'gentle Venetian girl to love Othello' and, more recently Kiernan Ryan has argued that all too often critics have underestimated Desdemona. Describing her as a character of 'formidable courage, passion and resolve', Ryan points out the nerve it would have needed for a woman in her position to flout the taboos of her society by marrying a black man.

In any critical evaluation of Desdemona, we must remember she's meant to be a very young woman, not really much more than a girl. Keeping this in mind might incline us to view her courage and strength of character more favourably.

Iago

What is it about Iago that has led to so much critical discussion of his character and disagreement in interpretation? Famously, the Romantic poet Samuel Taylor Coleridge wondered what motivated Iago's machinations, concluding that nothing Iago ever says is substantial enough to explain his malignity. On the other hand, as we shall see, some modern critics, such as Kiernan Ryan, claim that 'the truth is that nothing could be less mysterious than the source of Iago's malignity'. Whichever side you take, Iago's apparent elusiveness has certainly inspired critics, actors and directors to discover various, different sources for his villainy. Hence, among the many interpretations of his character he has been read and/or played as a vice figure from medieval morality plays, as a male witch, as a repressed homosexual, as a reactive puritan, as a mordant joker and as a psychopath and/or a sociopath. While some readers believe it is Iago's envy of Cassio and Othello's nobility that drives him to revenge, others argue that his revenge springs from a suppressed love of Desdemona. Whereas in the source material from Cinthio the Iago character had a clear and obvious motivation, this is missing from Shakespeare's characterisation, a deliberate gap or hole, a technique of absence that encourages different readers to fill it with their various interpretations and theories. What isn't in doubt, however, is that Iago is a powerfully disturbing and troubling character, a character with a brilliant mind intent on doing terrible harm to others and this makes him such a consistently compelling stage presence that some critics argue the play should really have been named after him.

Ostensibly, unlike Shakespeare's other Machiavellian villains, Iago does not appear to be motivated by a lust for power or to damage others as means to an increase in rank, status or power. Whereas Lady Macbeth divests herself of her female qualities to help her husband to the crown and Edmund in *King Lear* betrays his brother and father to climb the greasy pole and Claudius plans Hamlet's death to cling to the kingship, for Iago the destruction of Othello and Desdemona appears to be an end in itself. How could Iago benefit by Desdemona's murder? What would he gain through Othello's punishment for murdering

Desdemona? Nothing, it would seem. For Iago, the payoff for his crimes is perhaps the power he wields in reducing Othello and his love for Desdemona to rubble. Perhaps Iago is not after any worldly benefit; rather he makes others suffer because he enjoys the feeling of power it gives him. Fundamentally, then, perhaps Iago is best understood as a sadist. On the other hand, perhaps he makes them suffer so that they can feel what he has felt, such as the gnawing doubt about whether his wife has been unfaithful to him. Perhaps, then, Iago is best understood as someone seeking revenge.

Sympathy for the devil?

Is it possible to see things from Iago's perspective, even to forgive him to some extent for his villainy? Clearly, he is a malcontent with some grounds for feeling discontented with Venetian society and its values. This is a society in which rank and status are crucially important. But, despite his manifold talents and high intelligence, he has no opportunities to prosper or increase his status or fulfil his vast potential in the narrow world in which he exists. Even when he does loyal, sterling service, such as he has done for Othello on the battlefield, it will not necessarily be rewarded – it is Cassio who is promoted to a higher rank, not the more deserving Iago. And Cassio is not promoted because he is better qualified or has worked harder for it, but because he comes from a higher class. Adding insult to injury, despite being an outsider, Othello has been promoted to a general due to the service he has done for Venice. Hence it is perfectly understandable that Iago feels his merits have been ignored and he has been treated unjustly.

Additionally, rather than just accepting the injustices of the ways in which the Venetian world works, Iago sets about enterprisingly making up his own rules. Shakespeare was writing at a time when history was going through a mjoar change, with the old world of aristocratic authority and inherited ways of thinking being challenged by new more democratic and meritocratic forces and by the rise of commerce and science. In some ways, doesn't Iago, embody the new, modern, meritocratic, self-fashioning spirit? If in him an enterprisingly individualistic spirit is distorted and corrupted into doing evil, in part isn't this because of the ways in which entirely laudable impulses were stifled and thwarted by a world still clinging onto to the vestiges of aristocratic power? If we should feel sympathy for Othello as a cultural outsider and for Desdemona as a woman in a patriarchal world, mustn't we extend similar feelings to Iago as a class outsider in a culture divided rigidly by rank and status, governed by inherited power and driven by superficial courtly manners?

Iago lives in a world in which lusty fools like Roderigo are richer than he can ever hope to be and where hypocrites like Brabantio wield more legitimate power than he can ever hope to have. Like Hamlet, Iago understands that all's the world's a stage. He understands how his world really works and he sees through its hypocrisies. He is wise to the pretensions and pomposities, even of the supposedly noble characters, such as Othello and Cassio. Doubly betrayed by his master, Othello, underestimated and/or unjustly ignored by everyone else, he is an avenger who surely has every right to feel aggrieved. If we protest that he expresses racist and misogynistic views, a close study will reveal he only does so when manipulating other characters. Indeed, his strategies expose the racism and misogyny inherent in characters who otherwise might appear to be noble. Think, for instance, of how quickly Othello is prepared to believe Desdemona has been unfaithful to him.

You might protest that Iago uses the language of evil, calling up the forces of hell to make his plans prosper. But, in doing this he is like Hamlet calling up similar dark voices to force him to take his revenge. Like Hamlet, arguably Iago doesn't use this language because he is a devil, but as another form of rhetoric, a way of galvanising himself by drawing on imaginary forces in world in which he lacks any real power.

This sympathetic line of thinking can, however, only take us so far, of course. Certainly, thinking like this humanises Iago and makes him seem less like a devil. But it runs up against the malign form his revenge takes, his brutally callous treatment of Roderigo and Cassio and the cowardly killing of his own wife. To agree that Iago has sound reasons to feel aggrieved is not to agree necessarily with what he does about this injustice. Granted he has been mistreated by Othello, but the punishment Iago inflicts is obviously disproportionate. And what has Desdemona ever done to harm Iago? Nothing in the way he has been treated can justify his machinations against her.

Reading the world through Iago's eyes, coupled with the effect his seductive manipulative charisma can have on an audience, can take us dangerously close to excusing the behaviour of a human monster.

Grotesque epitome?

Like many other critics, A.C. Bradley assumed Iago's character defects were those of an exceptionally malign individual. Venetian society is, for these critics, essentially civilised and Iago is the dark exception hidden within. Countering Bradley, Kiernan Ryan argues that Iago is,  rather, a product of Venetian society, an embodiment, indeed, of its worst features. Iago's characteristics, Ryan suggests, are the 'widely shared products of the kind of culture Iago inhabits'. According to Ryan, rather than being a class outsider, Iago 'embodies a deep-rooted power-structure' and a 'concomitant view of the world' in its most 'virulent form'. The most disturbing thing about Iago, in this reading, is not that he's some kind of 'unfathomable psychopath' or uniquely ervil outlier, but that he's 'pathologically normal', 'terrifyingly typical' in fact, of his world. Iago embodies Venetian society in its most ruthless and destructive form. Reformulating the same idea, Ryan writes that Iago is not a 'monstrous deviation from the civilised Venetian norm, but the unmasked incarnation of its actual barbarity', not Venice's 'demonic antithesis' but, in fact, its 'grotesque epitome'.

As we have noted, Iago's plots are so effective because he exploits common ways of thinking, using his victims' own beliefs and cultural expectations against them. Other characters are so ready to believe him exactly because he is using commonly accepted ideas. For example, to ensnare and poison Othello, Iago uses toxic patriarchal assumptions about women he can rely on Othello sharing as a married man in the same society. Iago's debasing portrayal of women 'as lustful and devious shews and the bane of men's lives' is, Ryan argues, 'as old as patriarchy and as intrinsic to the play's Venetian world as racial prejudice'. In fact, so integral are sexist views to Venetian society that they have 'acquired proverbial force', as expressed in various couplets from the play. Hence Othello is so quick to believe in Iago's slander of Desdemona because he is already 'culturally primed to do so'. Through this manipulation and plotting Iago thus makes 'outward and visible that narratives that inwardly and invisibly grip people's minds', including, perhaps, his own.

In short, rather than being the monster or barbarian hidden within the folds of civilisation, Iago removes the mask of civility to reveal the truly monstrous and barbarous nature of that society.

Despite the focus on Iago as a malign product of a society, like other critics, Ryan seeks to identify a single key to unlock the enigma of his motivation. For Ryan the 'traumatic affronts to his self-regard' such as being passed over for promotion by the Florentine outsider, Cassio, are the 'mainspring to his iniquity'. Iago's 'intolerable feeling of interiority' drives his 'compulsion to prove himself secretly superior' to those that have debased him. Punishing other characters, Iago is putting them in place, i.e., as his subordinates. Hence the 'true objective' of his revenge is the 'degradation of his victims'. Returning to his central thesis, Ryan concludes that Iago's obsession with hierarchy and his [unjust] place within it and the anger and 'resentment of servitude' as well as his misogyny and racism have been 'bred into him' by a 'socially, racially and sexually divisive society'. For Ryan, Iago is a monster, but he has been made into one by Venetian society.

Playing Iago

How would you choose to play Iago? It's important to keep in mind when reading the play or watching a production that throughout the action Iago is always engaged in a mortally dangerous game. This jeopardy is, of course, part of the thrill of the game, both for us and for Iago himself and perhaps also partly explains his motivation. He has to keep so many plates both spinning and spinning separately from each other to avoid everything coming crashing down upon him. There are many, many occasions when his scheming could be undone by events and punishment dished out accordingly. Think, for instance, of the arrival of the trusted authority figure of Lodovico in Cyprus at a critical point in the play. Perhaps, noting the change in Othello's behaviour towards Desdemona, Lodovico will put two and two together. Or maybe not. For Iago there are, however, three principal sources of danger, namely Roderigo, Emilia and Othello.

All it would take, for instance, for his plans to collapse and disaster to come his way is for other characters to happen upon or overhearing him conspiring with Roderigo, particularly in Cyprus. In their interactions, Iago and Roderigo do not speak in code to mask their plans, nor do they meet in a secret, private place. In fact, Iago doesn't arrange to see Roderigo; rather Roderigo seems to pop up from time to time and Iago then has to deal with him there and then. There's a close shave in Act II, Sc. 3, for instance, when Roderigo arrives unexpectedly while Iago is talking to Montano about Cassio's weakness for booze. Iago seems startled by Roderigo's sudden appearance - 'How now, Roderigo!' - but manages to get rid of him quickly, within two lines and before Roderigo utters so much as a word, and before Montano notices him or asks any tricky questions. Another danger is that Roderigo will at some stage realise he is being duped and choose to expose Iago's villainy. Exasperated by being beaten and by getting no closer to Desdemona, Roderigo almost does so in Act IV, Sc. 2.

Long before she finally reveals her husband's machinations, Emilia has intuitions about a villain betraying her mistress. After Othello has called Desdemona a whore a little earlier in the same scene, Emilia says:

'I'll be hanged if some eternal villain,
Some busy and insinuating rogue,
Some cogging, cozening slave, to get some office,
Have not devised this slander.'

She a hair's breadth away from the truth. For the audience, already suffering from the play's prolonged use of dramatic irony, agonisingly close. Literally so - as she is saying these words Iago is standing right there beside her, probably trying to look innocent. If Emilia had made one connection here, probably Desdemona's death would have been avoided as well as Othello's, and her husband would have been punished for his lies. Unsurprisingly Iago is keen to shut down his wife's line of thought:

'Fie, there is no such man; it is impossible.'

But Emilia doesn't take the hint and carries on in the same vein: 'some most villainous knave / some base notorious knave, some scurvy fellow' must, she says, have 'abused' Othello's mind. Yes, quite right. Nail on the head. Exactly so. And who could that possibly be, Emilia? Suddenly Iago fears he will be exposed. Responding, this time he shifts into insults and tight-lipped imperatives - 'speak within door'; 'You are a fool. Go to'. In other words, 'shut the **** up'. Only when Desdemona intervenes and moves the conversation on to a different topic is Iago off the hook.

Imagine performing this scene. What looks does Iago give Emilia as she comes so close to realising the truth or in helping Desdemona to do so? When Iago tells her to shut up, does Emilia wonder why her husband is speaking to her like this, why he seems suddenly to be so agitated and angry? What looks does she give him? Is she beginning to suspect something or is Iago as adept at deceiving his wife and he is at hoodwinking everyone else? Directors and actors will have to decide.

But the greatest danger for Iago is Othello. Iago know he is playing tag with a tiger. And perhaps, for him, there's no greater, more exquisite sport than that. Or to put it another way, in the many conversations he has with his master in which he slowly insinuates Desdemona's infidelity with Cassio, Iago walks along the sharpest and most perilous of knife edges. All it might take to fall is for Othello to speak directly to Cassio or for Othello to have more trust in his wife than in his ancient or for his love for her to outweigh his suspicions or for him to wonder why Iago might be besmirching Desdemona's reputation or him to share what Iago tells him with someone he could really trust, such as Lodovico. Othello does,

indeed, consider the possibility that Iago is lying and makes it clear that if he is, he will be made to suffer horribly, 'thou hadst been better born a dog / than answer my waked wrath'. The stakes are high, this game is dangerous. But also so exhilarating.

To rachet up the dramatic tension even higher, Shakespeare ensures that, from time to time, Othello gets within a gnat's whisker of discovering the truth. For example, when Iago is casting aspersions about Cassio in Act III, Sc.3, Othello tells him that he 'dost conspire against thy friend'. True, just not in the way Othello means it. In the same exchange, Othello even calls Iago a 'villain': 'Villain, be sure thou prove my love a whore'. Yet more agonising dramatic irony. For Iago, the ever-present danger of discovery and the potential for terrible punishment only intensifies the fun.

Devilish shapeshifter

Iago plays many different roles in the play and does so with equal panache. A master of different discourses, he alters his words to suit the occasion and his interlocutor to bend them to his will. As Simon Palfrey writes, Iago is a corrupting agent whose words 'divide and conquer like cancerous cells'. Many critics have noted how Iago is also like a playwright or a puppeteer. Palfrey takes this further, opining that Iago is a kind of demon, a male succubus, 'stealing the mind and animating the body' of its victims. With a devilish power, Iago 'moves in and out of those he encounters, drawing from them, combining with them, taking them hostage' and making them his agents.

Iago's manipulation and 'hostage-taking' of other characters is mirrored by his control of us, his uneasy but complicit audience. From the start, we are dependent on him, not quite sure what is really going on, but entranced by his performance. From the get-go, as Palfrey notes, Iago 'establishes that there will be only one source of audience satisfaction: him, in good time, as he chooses'. Directing our understanding of other characters, turning us all into voyeurs, controlling the play's narrative, telling us whatever and whenever he wishes, he has us all – other characters, readers, audiences, actors, directors and critics - in his diabolically commodious pocket.

Cassio

On first impressions, Othello's one-time lieutenant, Cassio, might seem to be an honourable, smoothly well-mannered, noble character. Think, for instance, of how he refuses to be drawn into Iago's smuttily suggestive descriptions of Desdemona in Act II, expressing instead respect for both her and her marriage, or think of the steadfast loyalty he shows, even under duress, to Othello. But, beneath the smooth appearance lies a more uncertain and less likeable character. If we are inclined to read 'thrice-gentle', 'sweet' Cassio through Desdemona's admiring and partial eyes, we would do well to remember his heartless treatment of Bianca. Whether Bianca is or is not a prostitute, Cassio certainly exploits her and treats her feelings with arrogant and callous disregard. In his laddish conversation with Iago in Act IV, Sc. 1, for instance, he is dismissive of her love and scoffs at the thought of marriage: 'I marry her? What a customer?' Thinking nothing of ridiculing her affections for him, he objectifies Bianca as a cheap, common object, a 'bauble', a worthless something he can discard at his convenience.

Beloved by Bianca, loathed by Iago, Cassio is many things to many characters in *Othello*. To Iago he's an outsider, a dubious, florid Florentine, and, moreover, a useless soldier 'that never set a squadron in the field', a man who is 'mere prattle without practice' - or, to use a colloquial phrase, all mouth and no trousers. Iago says that Cassio is 'voluble', meaning that he talks excessively and claims, enviously, that he always lands on his feet, standing 'so eminently in the degree of … fortune'. There is a smooth easiness in the world about Cassio, 'the daily beauty in his life', that torments Iago and makes him feel 'ugly'. Until disgraced in his drunken episode, Cassio had been promoted and was deeply trusted by Othello. In return, Cassio thinks of himself as being close to his superior, praying for Othello's safety after being 'parted / With foul and violent tempest'. After Othello's death, Lodovico reveals a high regard for Cassio, depending on him to govern Cyprus. For her part, Desdemona describes him as 'valiant', an epithet more often reserved for Othello. Out of all the characters, she is the most generous in her epithets, calling him 'good Cassio', 'gentle Cassio', 'valiant Cassio'.

Who, then, is Cassio, and where does he come from? He starts life in Shakespeare's source, Cinthio's 1565 text *Un Capitano Moro*, as the unnamed corporal or 'Captain'. Shakespeare needs to find a name for this character, making a less-than-subtle point in choosing 'Cassio' - a name that comes directly from the Latin *cassius,* meaning 'hollow' or 'empty'. However, we'll argue here that this name isn't just a dismissal of his personality or his lack of military qualification, suggesting, instead, that his 'hollow' and 'empty' nature is a technique used to underline his vulnerability and, importantly, to create a dramatic parallel between his and Desdemona's experiences.

To understand Cassio's role, we'll start by looking at some of the changes Shakespeare made to Cinthio's source. Cinthio's squadron leader - or 'Captain' - is someone 'to whom the Moor was much affectioned', and we are told that Desdemona is kind to him to please her husband, especially given their great friendship. Desdemona pleads on his behalf after he is dismissed from his position, telling her husband that, since Othello and Cassio had been such good friends, it would be foolish to waste such a relationship. Shakespeare changes this to unbalance the relationship between Othello and Cassio. In the play, Othello very rarely speaks directly to him, only once requesting that 'Tomorrow with your earliest / Let me have speech with you', a conversation that never takes place as Cassio is stripped of his rank before it can do so. This is a curious almost-conversation, the awkward silence filling the space where Cinthio's close and mutually affectionate friendship stood. This is dramatically important; by taking away Othello's affection and loyalty to a fellow soldier, Iago has a blank puppet that is easier to operate. Moreover, by removing the idea that this tragedy is one of a great friendship, the dramatic focus is tightened on Iago and Othello.

In Cinthio's tale, Cassio is not caught up in a drunken brawl. He is, instead, deprived of his rank as he freely chooses to draw his sword upon a superior. Cinthio's Cassio has a genuine and specific failure of character and the fault for his actions lies with him. However, Shakespeare attributes Cassio's fighting to his drunkenness while on duty, as prompted by the opportunistic Iago. Making a character drunk is an interesting theatrical choice: through it, Shakespeare makes Cassio an unpredictable threat, given that his behaviour could make him go anywhere, do anything. This erratic, clumsy behaviour is not out of character, we suggest, but rather an extension of the kind of social naivety or perhaps arrogance

Cassio displays throughout the beginning of the play. For example, Cassio kisses Emilia upon their arrival in Cyprus, despite knowing that this will irritate Iago: 'Let it not gall your patience, good Iago, / That I extend my manners; 'tis my breeding / That gives me this bold show of courtesy', he instructs Iago, before making a performance of kissing Emilia, presumably without her indication or consent. Despite his superficially smooth manners, Cassio always seems liable to do something ill-judged. This 'could-do-anything' portrayal of Cassio makes him a dramatic *tabula rasa*, a blank-slate of a character whose identity develops in whichever direction Shakespeare needs to point him in order to best exploit and extract the desires, machinations, and plans of other characters.

Unpredictability is written into his back-story. Introduced via Iago's description of him in Act I, he is presented as a character with no discernible history. Cassio is, in fact, a 'hollow' shell ready to be given a history by the powerful forces within the plot. Whereas Othello's history is set out in shimmering and persuasive language, Cassio only receives a perfunctory background check from Iago: 'One Michael Cassio,' so he is described, '...A fellow almost damn'd in a fair wife, / That never set a squadron in the field, / Nor the division of a battle knows / More than a spinster'. Notice that Iago describes Cassio not as what he *is*, but by stating what he is *not*. He was *almost* married, but presumably didn't carry it through; he has *never* 'set a squadron', but we don't know what he *has* actually done through military service. Once again, the theme of the difficulty of discerning appearance from reality crops up. Cassio appears to be a chivalrous nobleman, an integral part of the Venetian establishment. But really he's a Florentine of uncertain background and of unproved military prowess.

What is the point of Cassio? We do learn some things about his character, such as his clumsy flirtatiousness, and we understand some of his struggles to fit in with his peers, especially given that they supposedly outrank him in experience and seniority. Therefore, 'hollow' and 'empty' might seem a little extreme, unfair even. However, his vulnerability, ambiguous history, and lack of social sophistication leave him dramatically vulnerable to be exploited by other characters in the play, and this is an important parallel that Cassio holds with Desdemona. Indeed, in a play that focuses so much on Desdemona as the proxy victim of Iago's manipulation, Cassio is often side-lined. But, like Desdemona, he's a victim both of Iago and of Othello.

The key difference between Cassio and Desdemona - clearly - is that Cassio survives. At the end of the play, he looks on as Othello discovers the manipulation that has been used against him: Othello is then stripped of his 'power' and his 'command ... and Cassio rules in Cyprus'. In learning of the full deception that has been worked against him, and in watching Othello make his own journey from ignorance to understanding, Cassio is allowed to achieve what Desdemona cannot, a redemption of character and reputation. Cassio, then, represents Desdemona's other possible storyline, a path that she was never allowed to take. Both are exploited by the same men, and both seek an emotional connection with Othello that is either denied to them or is corrupted. In Cinthio's tale, however, Cassio never discovers the deception against him, making Shakespeare's changes more purposeful since Cassio discovers a truth that Desdemona never can. Cinthio's Captain - Cassio's source equivalent - has his leg cut off by the Iago under cover of darkness, who in turn tells the corporal that it was actually the Moor. This knowledge is used against Othello, who ends up being killed by Desdemona's family. Shakespeare actively changes his source material to give Cassio a clear conclusion and a greater understanding of events. Perhaps, then, this is why we should imagine that Cassio starts off the play living up to his 'hollow' or 'empty' name, not so much because of his superficiality or lack of social understanding, but because he is given a highly significant journey from disgrace to high status: where once he was empty and lacking in friends, he is now filled with the truth of events, and the potential for a long and successful career.

Emilia

To what extent is Emilia to blame for her mistress' death and to what extent does her eventual confession of her role in it redeem her as a character? For most of the play, Emilia's awkwardly dual roles of Desdemona's maid and Iago's wife mean that, though she doesn't fully understand the situation, her loyalties are, in fact, split in diametrically opposing directions. This lack of understanding raises questions about her culpability. Of course, she is married to the villain Iago, but until the end she does not appear to realise the full extent of his evil. On the other hand, she does know that her husband is 'wayward', and that he must have some mischievous project in mind, for he 'hath a hundred times / Woo'd [her] to steal' Desdemona's handkerchief. 'What he will do with it / Heaven knows, not I', she says rather disingenuously in Act III, adding weakly, 'I nothing but to please his fantasy'. But, she'd have to be a complete fool not to have any inkling that Iago's intentions are less than benign. On the other hand, it's only in Act V that she realises the full horror of these less-than-benign intentions.

For much of the play, as would be expected of her, Emilia is most loyal to her husband. Shakespeare goes to some pains to emphasise Emilia's keenness to please Iago by giving him what he wants. But she also expresses a wish to wipe her hands clean of the consequences. Her statement of ignorance - 'Heaven knows, not I' - occupies an entire line of iambic pentameter and the emphatic metre, followed by portentous silence, indicate some awareness that his intentions are not good. It sounds like a weak excuse. It sounds like

Emilia is wilfully shutting her eyes to the consequences of her own actions. It sounds like she doesn't want to think too deeply about the true nature of the man she has married. However, upon Iago 'snatching' the handkerchief, she appears to have a mini crisis of conscience, asking him that 'If it be not for some purpose of import' to give it back to her. Note that she does not chide against a malicious or 'wayward' purpose for the handkerchief, instead only asking that he should give it back if it is *unimportant*. This choice of wording is significant. *Take it if it will serve your purpose,* she is saying here: a protest that is not really a protest at all, in fact, and one which seems even to take some pleasure in the idea of what is to come.

The play is ambiguous about Emilia's role in, and the extent of her culpability for, Desdemona's death. Her complicity in Iago's behaviour seems to be the kind of character flaw that creates Othello's downfall - that of being too trusting and uncritical of others - or perhaps her weakness is a desire for passive cruelty, of allowing the worst to happen whilst protesting that she could not have been its cause. Or perhaps there is just something desperate about her love for Iago and her desire to please him. Though when we see them together, Iago only ever treats her with undisguised contempt, through being this kind of proxy for her husband, in effect, despite her apparently genuine concern for her welfare, Emilia actively betrays her mistress.

However, her actions also create an uncomfortable, intimate connection between the two women: they are both exploited by Iago in pursuit of Othello's downfall, they both die at the hands of their husbands. The closeness of their role is underlined by the fact that, whilst there are many scenes where only men speak to each other, Desdemona and Emilia are the only two women who speak alone together on stage. The play has what is called a *homosocial* environment - an environment made up of a single gender - which aligns Emilia more closely with Desdemona as we move towards the end of the play. Shakespeare draws our attention to the question of Emilia's responsibility and complicity in Desdemona's death when Desdemona instructs her to 'Lay on my bed my wedding sheets, remember, / And call my husband hither': the wedding sheets, of course, in which Desdemona shall later die. Earlier, Emilia carries out Iago's instructions knowing that he has ill intentions of some sort. Here, she must carry out instructions again, but this time she is ignorant of the play's wider plan for these 'wedding sheets', her lack of knowledge aligning her more closely with her mistress and making her seem less culpable for her death.

Shakespeare uses dramatic irony to underscore Emilia's ignorance. Shocked by how Othello is now speaking of Desdemona, bewildered, she asks 'why should he call her whore?' At this point, she is entirely unaware of her husband's role in the sullying of Desdemona's reputation. But, she almost hits on the truth when she surmises that 'the Moor's abused by some most villainous knave, / Some base notorious knave, some scurvy fellow'. This is an intelligent and correct perception, but it's undermined by the fact that the very same knave is standing right there beside her. A classic character arc tends to see an individual develop from a state of ignorance to experience, from naivety to wisdom. Yet, at this stage of the play, Emilia has gone from a state of knowing her husband is 'up to something' to, apparently, having no concept that the villain who has abused both her mistress and Othello sleeps in her bed.

Too late the penny finally drops for Emilia to save Desdemona, but it does allow her to achieve some degree of redemption for her role in her death. Having been sent to apprise Othello of Cassio's injury and Roderigo's death, in Act V, Sc. 2 she discovers Desdemona dying and Othello in a trance-like state. Angrily Emilia protests her mistress' angelic innocence and lambasts Othello for his hellish murder. Prefiguring the anagnorisis that will finally remove the blindfold from Othello's eyes, she is stopped in her tracks when Othello tells her he had hard proof of Desdemona's unfaithfulness from her husband. The awful truth takes a moment to hit home:

EMILIA: My husband?
OTHELLO: Thy husband.

It is a bitter pill she finds almost impossible to swallow: Three times she can only repeat the same two astonished words. She cannot accept it. She doesn't want it to be true. The fourth time she repeats it, she tries to make everything as clear as possible, so there can be no room for any doubt: 'My husband says that she was false?'

This revelation is the tipping point for Emilia and, arguably, begins her redemption. Instantly her loyalty swings away from Iago and towards her dying mistress. Now, she doesn't hesitate or hold back: 'may his pernicious soul / Rot half a grain a day. He lies to th'heart.' Perhaps she has always known this or at least feared this about her husband. Perhaps she has been in deep denial about his true nature. Perhaps there was part of her envious of Desdemona and wishing her some sort of harm. Perhaps, perhaps. But released now and guilty, despite Othello threatening her with his sword, immediately she cries out for help. And among those rushing in to see what has happened is her husband, Iago.

Despite everything, Emilia still gives him a chance to deny everything. But he does not. So, by duty she is 'bound to speak' of what she knows, though Iago warns her to shut up – to 'charm' her tongue and twice warns her to 'get you home'. But, Emilia is beyond his control now and will not be silenced: 'No, I will speak as liberal as the north…/ …let the all / All, all cry shame against me, yet I'll speak'. And once she has confessed that she stole the handkerchief, in the general confusion Iago seizes the opportunity to stab his wife in the back. So much for marital loyalty.

In addition to paralleling Desdemona, through their marriages and deaths at the hands of their husbands, Emilia plays an important role as an opposite, or foil, to her mistress. Whereas Desdemona is an ingenue character, young and essentially innocent, Emilia is older and more worldly-wise. In their conversation in Act IV, Sc. 3 they express starkly opposing views of women and of marriage. Desdemona cannot believe that any woman would abuse her husband in the ways that husbands sometimes abuse their wives, for by 'this heavenly light' she would never be unfaithful. Neither would I, Emilia retorts sharply, but 'I might do't as well i'th'dark'. Again, Desdemona's lofty idealism is undercut by Emilia's down-to-earth realism: whereas Desdemona says she would not commit adultery for 'all the world', Emilia counters with 'who would not make her husband a cuckold to make him a monarch?' Indeed, she'd go further, even braving 'purgatory for't'.

Emilia is then given her longest speech in the play, some 20 lines and, as Kiernan Ryan points out, it's an important and radical intervention. In this speech, Emilia directly confronts and calls into question some of the key presuppositions underpinning the play: Rather than infidelity being the fault of women, for instance, who, in accord with masculine concepts of honour, must therefore be punished for it, Emilia boldly counters that 'it is their husbands' faults /. If wives do fall'. She then lists myriad ways in which husbands commonly mistreat their wives. Although she speaks in generalising non-personal terms, implying this sort of mistreatment is universal, hovering in the background here, unspoken, is her own marriage and her own ghastly husband. Powerfully Emilia asserts the feelings and agency of women, warning husbands that their ill treatment of their wives will be revenged upon them. Ryan argues that Emilia shows she understands that the supposed 'laws of conscience' are not natural, but man-made and are only made to seem natural through custom, and hence that such laws can be changed. For Ryan, the line of argument Emilia develops 'cuts the ground from under the misogynistic views of wives and women', framing the tragedy as a patriarchal one, the 'product of that kind of culture at that time rather than the timeless tragedy of the human condition'. In effect, then, Emilia becomes in these 20 lines a mouthpiece for Shakespeare himself.

Minor characters

Roderigo

He's a desperate eejit of a character, isn't he, Roderigo? What an utter wally. But, indeed, in the end, also far worse than that. If he hadn't been persuaded to try to kill Cassio in cold blood in Act V, perhaps we might even have had some pity for Roderigo. Up until that point, yes, he was a fool and a desperate one at that, but he didn't really mean anyone any harm. Repeatedly duped by Iago into giving him gold and jewels in a desperately ill-advised, forlorn and utterly misguided attempt to win Desdemona's attention, he is a particularly pathetic version of the unrequited lover, driven almost crazy by a love that is not returned. As such, Roderigo is another vehicle for Shakespeare to dramatize the potential torments of love, or of lust. But, in conspiring in a cowardly attempted murder, Roderigo turns himself also into a villain, a word he helplessly keeps repeating as he lies dying from his stab wounds, the final mortal one being delivered by a man he trusted and supposed to be his ally.

He might have been a very wealthy Venetian gentleman and he might have gone to incredible lengths to try to win Desdemona's heart, such as engaging Iago to help him and travelling perilously to Cyprus to pursue her, but, from the start of the play, we know he is far from being a suitable match. For one thing, Brabantio has already told him in 'honest plainness' that his daughter is 'not for thee'. Moreover, it is quickly established in Act I, Sc. 1 that he is a fool who will be easily manipulated by Iago, an impression that is confirmed in all their subsequent interactions. Yes, love and jealousy may have driven him to distraction, like Othello, but as a foil for the general Roderigo only highlights

Othello's manifold noble qualities through his own singular lack of them. Whereas Othello wins Desdemona's heart with his eloquence and with his courage, for instance, Roderigo cannot pluck up the courage even to speak to her directly. Indeed, in the play, he hardly speaks to anyone other than Iago.

As well as providing the semi-comic spectacle of the pitiful distracted lover, desperate enough to drown himself, he claims, from unrequited love, through Roderigo Shakespeare further exposes Venetian society and its values. If Roderigo embodies the average Venetian gentleman, it might explain why Desdemona rejected all of them for Othello. Roderigo is, for instance, casually and horribly racist - witness his descriptions of Othello as 'the thick-lips' and as the 'lascivious Moor'. Despite his obvious disdain for Roderigo, once he believes Desdemona has run off with Othello, Brabantio wishes that he 'had had her' instead. This reaction to discovering his daughter gone reveals the wide extent of the racism and hypocrisy lying just beneath the surface of supposedly civilised Venetian culture.

Shakespeare entirely invented the character of Roderigo and uses him to reveal Iago's villainous character; Iago is so contemptuous of him than he doesn't bother to hide his true nature. As well as a fool for Iago, Roderigo is also a foil for the villain. Through contrast, his stupidity and credulity emphasise Iago's cynical intelligence. Roderigo is also an opportunity, but also a constant danger for Iago. On the one hand, he is a useful, pliant tool, one Iago employs to good effect when rousing Brabantio and in first enraging and later wounding Cassio. On the other hand, Roderigo could at any point spill the beans. He is in on the Iago's conspiracies and from the start is the only character who knows that Iago's apparent loyalty and service to Othello is a sham. Like other characters, Roderigo doesn't, however, put two and two together. Although Iago tells him that he is using Othello only to serve his own ends, Roderigo fails to realise he is being deceived and exploited by the same man. This is further evidence of his foolishness and perhaps how his love/lust for Desdemona blinds him to reason. Nevertheless, despite being a fool, Roderigo needs to be carefully managed by Iago and also eventually disposed of mercilessly, when the opportunity arises.

Bianca

Many critics have argued that the nature of the relationship between the three female characters in the play is based on a contrast of timeless stereotypes of women. Virginia Mason Vaughan, for instance, has identified Desdemona as representing the 'chaste bride', Emilia the 'earthy matron' and Bianca as 'the prostitute'. Though her name means whiteness, sexually impure Bianca is often interpreted to function as an opposite to the pure and virginal Desdemona. However, in some ways the two women are linked. Although they never appear on stage in a scene together, they are connected, for example, by their handling of the handkerchief. The fact that Bianca seems unable to copy it has led some critics to argue this is because the handkerchief is a symbol of a pure, valid marriage. So, there is a pattern of both insistent differences between Desdemona as well as troubling similarities.

At first glance, Bianca seems to be the opposite of Desdemona and does everything that Desdemona is wrongly accused of doing. She is Cassio's mistress and openly expresses the kind of sexuality for which Desdemona is shamed. Although the accusation that she is a courtesan, a 'strumpet', portrays her as the opposite to Desdemona, it also strongly aligns her, however, with Desdemona in our minds, since Desdemona is the only other character to be labelled a 'whore'. In Bianca, we have then a visual representation of Othello's worst nightmare for what Desdemona *could* be, but isn't.

What stance does this play take on Bianca, a character who embodies a destructive stereotype of women? Is it a little generous to claim that

Shakespeare is trying to make us feel sympathy for Bianca? Certainly, she's treated callously by Cassio and more cruelly still by Iago. But she's also a dupe, like Roderigo, taken in by Cassio's charm. Overall, she's not a very developed character and so it is hard for the audience to fully invest in her feelings. What then is the point of her presence in the play?

The answer - or one of the answers - lies in the fact that Bianca's jealousy over Cassio's supposed infidelity is the only example of a woman being outspokenly jealous over a male partner in this play. Othello and Bianca are thus curiously linked in this way. Both are hot-tempered, and both are willing to believe that the handkerchief represents infidelity, Bianca describing it as 'some token from a newer friend'. Yet, whilst jealous Othello moves to kill Desdemona, jealous Bianca returns unquestioningly to Cassio in his injury, tending to his safety and publicly declaring her allegiance to him. Bianca is therefore the play's example of a jealousy that can pass on the wind, of an envy that doesn't have to completely consume one person in order to destroy someone else. Because of this, her relatively minor storyline has a major impact upon our judgement of Othello, who made the other, poorer choice.

The Duke of Venice & Lodovico

There are two opposite ways of reading and playing the Duke of Venice, a character who in some productions doubles up as Brabantio's kinsman,

Lodovico. Either the Duke can be played as a wise and gracious authority figure who listens to Brabantio's ravings about Othello in Act I with admirable equanimity and, moreover, delivers a just judgement in Othello's favour, or he can be read/played as a not-too-subtle politician, most keen to exploit Othello's military prowess in the defence of Cyprus.

Initial impressions suggest the former. In welcome contrast to the hostile and racist language used about Othello by other characters, when the Duke first addresses his general at the Senate, his tone is one of admiration: 'Valiant Othello'. Dealing with Brabantio's accusations, the Duke then allows both Othello and Desdemona to speak for themselves and when Brabantio insists at length that Othello must have used drugs and/or witchcraft to beguile his daughter, the Duke remains disinterested and unpersuaded; 'To vouch this is no proof'. It seems that the Duke's pseudo-court will proceed rationally, not racially. The Duke also recognises the persuasive power of Othello's account of his wooing of Desdemona, telling Brabantio, frankly, that the tale would 'win' his daughter too, he listens to what Desdemona has to say for herself and arbitrates between the parties justly.

What's not to like? Well, for modern readers, the Duke's apparent compliment that Othello is 'far more fair than black' is highly problematic, as it perpetuates racist ideas about whiteness equating to goodness and blackness to evil. If we accept the arguments of critics such as Kiernan Ryan that the violent toxicity of the play originates in the norms and values of Venice, then that must implicate the character who most embodies and, indeed, enforces those norms and values, the Duke. Unsurprisingly, Ryan interprets the Duke's character unsympathetically, arguing, for instance, that his use of 'mollifying platitudes are motivated by the Senate's overriding need for Othello to defend Cyprus'.

Actually, Ryan wrote that sentence about Lodovico and in his essay on *Othello* treats the two as if they are the same character. However, when Lodovico arrives on Cyprus in Act IV, Sc.1 it is the first time his name has been used in the play and while the way he refers to the Duke could be read as speaking about himself royally in the third person – 'the Duke and senators of Venice greet you' – it seems peculiar that he then hands Othello a letter from the Duke, rather than just speaking for himself. Othello responds by referring to 'their pleasure' rather than 'your', indicating that he doesn't treat Lodovico as if he is the Duke. Meanwhile Desdemona calls him her cousin and, if further corroboration is required, speaking about the letter Lodovico says 'I think, they [the writers of the letter] 'do command him home'. Odd for him not to know the content, if he wrote this letter himself.

Perhaps the conflation of the two characters stems from the fact that in some productions they are played by the same actor and because both are clearly figures of authority. But Lodovico does seem to be a different man from the Duke. As Ryan himself says, picking up Desdemona's admiring comment that 'this Lodovico is proper man', this character epitomises the 'many noble matches Desdemona forsook to marry Othello'. Putting the conflation to one side, Lodovico's arrival in Cyprus is a symbol of the potential for order to be restored on the island and, as such, a threat to Iago's scheming. Recognising this danger, Iago moves swiftly to assure Lodovico that Othello is 'much changed' and, like everyone else Lodovico, is taken in by Iago's act, a mistake emphasised a few scenes later when he immediately trusts Iago's account of the fight and refers to him as a 'very valiant fellow'. Nevertheless, Lodovico is clearly shocked at Othello's mistreatment of Desdemona and as such is a character who could either interrogate Othello about why he is treating his wife so badly, or indeed, be a character to whom Othello could, potentially, confide.

As a figure of authority, Lodovico has the potential to bring justice and to prevent calamity. But, duped by Iago, he is unable to fulfil this potential and dispenses justice only when it is too late. In his last appearance in the play, it is Lodovico who delivers Othello's anagnorisis, revealing to him the extent of Iago's villainy and Cassio's innocence, but he fails to anticipate how these shocks will affect Othello. Lodovico's attempts to issue commands, including one to arrest Othello, are undermined when Othello chooses to kill himself rather than be imprisoned. Lodovico's attempts to shame the defiantly mute Iago, in the play's concluding lines, are similarly ineffective. All that is left for Lodovico to do is to order the corpses to be 'hid' from sight, for Othello's fortunes to be seized and for appropriate torture to be inflicted on Iago. Having made these commands, he's back off home to Venice, in order to relate this 'heavy act' with a 'heavy heart'. Somehow, that doesn't seem entirely adequate.

Montano and Gratiano

Both these characters play very minor roles in the play, so we're not going to worry too much about them. **Montano,** of course, is the Governor of Cyprus and, as such, another leading authority figure. Notably, he is happy to cede his leadership role to Othello when he arrives on the island in Act II. Our understanding of characters is produced by a combination of how they appear in the play with what others say about them. In this respect, Montano adds to our impressions of Othello and his standing in Venetian culture. Countering earlier negative representations, as the Duke has done, Montano expresses admiration and respect for Othello. Rather than referring to his character in racial terms, Montano focuses instead on the strengths of Othello's personality, calling him 'brave Othello', commending him as a 'worthy governor' and commenting warmly on how he 'commands / Like a full soldier'.

In his subsequent conversation with Iago, Montano repeats similar sentiments, referring to Othello's 'good nature' and calling him 'the noble Moor'. The fact that this time, although expressing admiration, Montano falls into the habit of describing Othello as 'the Moor' shows how ubiquitous such racialised thinking is in the world of the play. It is also worth noting that though Roderigo makes a brief appearance during this conversation, Montano has no doubts about Iago's trustworthiness. He accepts at face value what Iago tells him about Cassio. Montano is yet another character who listens to Iago and swallows his poison.

Montano, of course, is injured, nearly fatally, in the fight with Cassio in Act II. He is also used then by Iago to advance his schemes and by Shakespeare to expose the dangerous side of Cassio. For Iago, the fight kills two birds with one stone: helpfully removing from Othello the support of an important authority figure in Montano, it also banishes Cassio, leaving Othello more vulnerable and exposed and more dependent on Iago's counsel.

Returning in the final scene of the play, having benefitted presumably from some expert surgery, Montano is part of the group who discover Desdemona's murder and Iago's villainy. When Othello tries to kill Iago, it is Montano who 'disarms him' somehow. His full recovery is also suggested by the way he takes command of the situation, issuing orders to track down Iago and to guard Othello. It is interesting that in this speech that Montano refers to Othello as just 'the Moor' and Iago as a 'notorious villain', the start, perhaps, of a convenient reframing of their story. Notable too is that when Lodovico arrives on the scene, Montano steps back to allow him to take charge.

Unless he has been hiding on Cyprus from the beginning, presumably **Gratiano** arrives on the island with Lodovico in Act IV as one of his attendants. If this is true, it suggests Gratiano is of lower rank – he is not introduced, he has no lines and is only an 'attendant'. The impression is confirmed by his secondary role in the action of Act V. For most of the final scene he is less an active agent in the action and more a helpful commentator on it, performing a choric like role: Desdemona's 'father's dead'; 'The woman [Emilia] falls. Sure he hath killed his wife'; 'he's gone, but his wife's killed'. However, though he's a minor character and of lower status than Lodovico, he is still part of the power structure of Venice, as revealed by Lodovico ordering him to guard Othello's house and to 'seize upon the fortunes of the Moor'. These fortunes are, Lodovico declares, rightfully belong now to Gratiano, presumably because he is Brabantio's brother and Desdemona's uncle. In the light of this, we might think Gratiano's response to discovering his niece murdered a little underwhelming. He utters just two words, 'Poor Desdemon', before his sympathy shifts to how her death would have affected his brother and doesn't mention her again. Finally, it is also worth noting how power and status in Venice is tightly distributed among just a few male relations, like a political dynasty: Gratiano is not only the brother of a Senator, he is also kin to the high-ranking Lodovico.

Critical reception

The assessment objectives at A-level specifically refer to both the contexts of production and of *reception* of literary works. The ways in which *Othello* has been received and critiqued over the past 400 years have changed massively as the historical, cultural and social contexts in which the play is read and performed have changed. This commentary will explore the notable individual critical voices as well as the theoretical frameworks, such as new historicism, feminism and post-colonialism, through which the play has been viewed and reviewed.

Let's start by considering early views of the play. Thomas Rymer [1693] was unimpressed with various aspects of the play. As we've already noted in our section on props, he was particularly withering about Shakespeare's use of the handkerchief. Dismissing the play's characters as unbelievable, Rymer claimed the play was 'a bloody farce' as it does not have a moral lesson and because Desdemona lacks sense for marrying 'a blackamoor'. He also rejected *Othello* as a tragedy because it does not fit the neoclassical prescription of a play tracing the events of a single day in a single location. Many subsequent critics have also criticised the structure of *Othello*, especially what has come to be known as its 'double time scheme'. This phrase refers to the fact that though some aspects of the play imply the action takes place over a short period of a few days, others imply the characters are on Cyprus for far longer. In particular, Iago convinces Othello that Desdemona has been unfaithful to him on many separate occasions. [A modern critic, Kiernan Ryan, while agreeing that the play's time scheme is 'flagrantly incoherent', argues that this a strength, as the short amount of time spent on Cyprus makes Desdemona's infidelities impossible.]

Dr Johnson [1765] viewed *Othello* far more favourably than Rymer, praising the 'beauties of this play' as an example of 'Shakespeare's skill in human nature'. Johnson celebrated the portrayal of Othello as 'magnanimous, artless, and credulous, boundless in his confidence, ardent in his affection, inflexible in his resolution, and obdurate in his revenge'. Johnson also opposed Rymer's view by asserting that the play did indeed have a clear moral, viz 'not to make an unequal match'.

The era of Romanticism brought further interpretations, reflecting how textual readings reflect the social constructions and ideologies of their time. Samuel Taylor Coleridge [1819] praised Shakespeare's characters and did not dismiss Othello as some previous critics had, recognising him instead as 'a high and  chivalrous Moorish chief' whose actions are not the product of uncontrollable emotions but rather, a sense of moral indignation and wounded honour. Coleridge's criticism includes a particular fascination with Iago, who he describes has a 'passionless character' whose lack of rational justification for his revenge makes him a 'being next to Devil'. According to Coleridge, Iago's final soliloquy is best understood as 'the motive hunting of motiveless malignity'. This description remains one of the most famous interpretations of Iago's character and influenced future critical interpretations for generations. Nineteenth-century understanding of Shakespeare's characters, particularly that of Coleridge, was based on the belief that the characters expressed fundamental truths about human nature. Whilst the focus of criticism tends to stay with Othello and Iago, this increased awareness of characters as constructs encouraged greater critical interest in Desdemona.

Critical attention on the play's tragic heroine intersected with the growing number of women's voices in the realm of literary criticism. For example, Anna Jameson [1794-1860] wrote the first substantial volume discussing Shakespeare's female characters, *Characteristics of Women, Moral, Poetical, and Historical* [1832] – later retitled, rather more snappily, *Shakespeare's Heroines*. Jameson argued that Desdemona's plight, rather than Othello's, is the essence of the tragedy, suggesting that Desdemona's main features are her goodness and 'gentleness which not only cannot resent – but cannot resist'.

One of the leading critics to emerge in the early twentieth century was A. C. Bradley [1904], whose analysis of *Othello* was overwhelmingly positive. He saw love as the leading theme in the play and, for him, Othello is 'the most romantic figure among Shakespeare's heroes'. Arguing that Othello's murderous violence does not spring from his innate savagery, as some racist readings of the tragic hero had argued, but from the impossible situation he is in, Bradley also suggests Othello's jealousy is credible and stems from how recent his marriage was. Bradley believed the audience feels 'admiration' for Othello  and argued that the play is a celebration of 'the power of love and man's inconquerable mind'.

This sympathetic view of Othello, however, was strongly rejected by other leading twentieth century critics, most notably T. S. Eliot and F. R. Leavis. T.S. Eliot [1927] believed that Othello is self-dramatic and that his all-consuming jealousy demonstrates, at the end of the play, a 'terrible exposure of human weakness'. Similarly, F. R. Leavis [1952] disagreed with Bradley's reading, claiming instead that Othello was responsible for his own downfall, that his character was weak, and that this weakness is exposed as 'the stuff of which he is made begins at once to deteriorate'. Arguing that Othello is ignorant, Leavis lambasts the tragic hero's 'ferocious stupidity' and 'insane, self-deceiving passion'. Leavis also offers his interpretation of Iago, suggesting that his motivation is explained as 'a not uncommon kind of grudging malice'.

Later in the twentieth century criticism, attention shifted to language-focused analysis. This approach is evident, for instance, in the work of G. Wilson Knight [1930], who coined the term 'the Othello music' [as you might recall we mentioned in our section on Shakespeare's language]. Although he admired Othello's way of speaking, Knight argued that Othello 'loves emotion for emotion's sake' and Knight's criticism focuses on close analysis of language, which is sublime, he suggests, but also insincere. Helen Gardner offered a different interpretation in her essay 'The Noble Moor' [1955]. Rebutting Leavis' judgement, Gardner argued that Desdemona's murder has 'a stamp of the heroic' and that Othello deserves heroic status because he acted from inner necessity.

The twentieth century also brought a marked increase in feminist approaches to *Othello*. Moving on from Jameson's critical views, Marilyn French [1982] explored how the play is constructed on a misogynistic value system and, although Desdemona seemingly asserts herself and her desires early in the play, she ultimately 'accepts... that she must be obedient to males'. Lisa Jardine [1983] also examined Desdemona's character through a feminist lens, suggesting that the drama is wholly masculine and Desdemona's 'too-independent' character gives way to 'exemplary passivity in adversity' at the end, as she reverts to the stereotype of female behaviour and is punished by the patriarchy for her earlier independent thought and actions.

Building on the work of feminist critics such as French and Jardine, Ania Loomba [1987] added a post-colonial perspective, broadening the explorations of gender representations in *Othello* to also consider race and religion. Loomba examined the structures of oppression and Othello's positioning as a 'total outsider', as his 'colour and gender make him occupy contradictory positions in relation to power'. Loomba explored how Othello's relationship with Desdemona marginalises him from society and 'catalyses the contradictions in Othello's self-conception'. Loomba's criticism begins to take on what is called an intersectional approach, considering racism within the context of patriarchy and arguing for the importance of dismantling of oppressive ideologies.

New critical interpretations of *Othello* continue to emerge. New historicist critics, for instance, are interested in the way the play has been read and re-read over time. These critics highlight that, whilst the play has become a vehicle for discussions about race and racism, contemporary conceptualisations were only just emerging. Comments like the Duke's, 'far more fair than black' reveals racism when seen through the lens of our current societal understanding and certainly establishes his liminal position, although the play's contemporary audience – new historicists argue – would not have seen the play as directly focused on race in the same way. Critics such as Sean McEvoy also frame Othello's tragedy in historical terms, arguing that Othello lives according to a set of stories that have been superseded. Essentially, they

146

argue, that Othello's tragedy stems from the fact that he is still trying to live the life of a chivalric warrior in a world that is modernising and has become run by money and self-interest.

One notable example of new trends in critical approaches is the field of geo-political research. M. Christofides' *Othello's Secret* [2016] challenges conventional views of Othello as a Venetian play and argues that the domestic and military tensions in the play are precursors to Cyprus' more recent wars and divisions. Christofides' work provides new ways of seeing the play's setting and characters, as he suggests that 'Othello's problem is and always has been the problem of Cyprus'. Christofides' points out that, although four of the five Acts are set in Cyprus, academic studies of the play have tended to exclude discussion of the 'diverse, polycultural' ways in which the island is portrayed.

Critical interpretations of *Othello* are multiple, complex and ongoing. Often, indeed, critics clash over different, contradictory interpretations of the play. If you are studying the play at A-level, you should be well-informed of different ways of reading the play and about major landmarks in criticism. But that, alone, is not enough. The crucial thing is that you use different readings to develop and refine your own interpretations. One tip for examinations is that it is often more useful to find critics and criticism you strongly disagree with than that with which you already concur.

Teaching & revision ideas

Whichever board's exams you'll be taking, a fundamental part of the test will be your knowledge of the play. Check this by trying to write out a summary of the play, scene by scene, without using the script. Try to write no more than a couple of sentences for any one scene. Once you're done, compare it to other versions. Now choose a memorable title for each scene, as if were a chapter from a novel. The first scene, for example, could be called 'Darkness and Duplicity'. Then pick one quotation that you think best summarises this scene.

How many scenes are there in the play overall? Work out how many there are in each Act and then check against our tally on p. 148.

Now try to write out the narrative of the play in continuous prose using only about one side of A4.

A few pages on is our list of chapter-style titles for each scene of the play. However, there's been some strange eruption to their state and the order has been scrambled. How quickly can you put them back in the right sequence? How do our suggested titles compare to yours? [If you wish to check the correct sequence for these scenes is on p.162.]

Write out each scene title on a separate piece of paper and arrange in a pile, face down. Mix them together. Pick up one piece of paper and explain either to yourself or a partner in as much detail as possible exactly what happens in this scene. If you're a bit hazy, go back to the play and remind yourself. Take another piece of paper and repeat the process.

Mix the pieces of paper together and turn them over again. Now arrange them in the correct sequence as quickly as you can. Write out the sequence as a timeline. Add extra details, such as where the soliloquies fall, and key moments in the plot.

A similar exercise can be done to consolidate your knowledge of characters and their relationships to each other. Write out the name of every character who appears in the play on a separate piece of paper, turn face down and place in a pile. Now pick up any three pieces of paper at random. Put two of the characters together and separate the third, giving as many reasons for your pairing as you can. Then try to make a different pairing using the same three characters. Once you've exhausted what you have to say, place the pieces in the pile and start again. 10-15 minutes of this exercise, completed regularly, will really help secure your knowledge of all the play's dramatis personae and their relationships with each other.

For each of the play's main characters complete a character circle. This is a diagram in the form of concentric circles. Using a page of A4 paper write the character's name in the middle and around that write words they would use to describe themselves. Draw a circle around that and write down words other characters might use to describe them. Draw a circle around that and write in words critics have written or might write about the character. Draw another circle and add different interpretations of the character in various productions you've seen. In the remaining space write down any further thoughts you have about the character.

Minor, unnamed characters can slip under the radar of our critical attention. Tracking them, however, can often be a useful and incisive way of re-reading the text, one that can open new perspectives. Albeit always rather out of the spot-light of dramatic attention, in the background are various unnamed characters, such as the senators, officer, gentleman, musicians, the clown. Make a list of all the play's unnamed characters and check exactly which scenes they appear and what they say. What would be lost if all or any these characters were cut from the play?

Imagine you have been asked to direct an abridged version of *Othello*. Which scenes, or sections within scenes, could you cut and why? Once you've decided on these cuts to the play, try to make a strong counterargument about why they really should be retained. For example, does the play really need Act I? Verdi's opera, *Otello,* dispense with it. What's lost by this cut? A less major bit of editorial surgery might delete the opening of Act III, sc. 4 when Desdemona talks to the clown before Othello questions her about the lost handkerchief. Again, consider what would be lost by such a cut.

All narratives feature characters being frustrated in their pursuit of something they think they really want or need. Consider character motivations and objectives in this play. Pick any scene from the play and write down all the characters within it. Then for each character decide on what you consider to be their overall, most important objective for the whole play. Next write down their objective in this scene. Now zoom further in and consider what might be motivating their behaviour in each interaction they have with other characters. Notice the points at which it is easier and harder to decide what is motivating a character. To what extent are these motivations hidden from the other characters? Which characters are the most transparent and which are the most opaque?

Focus on the inner Iago, how his thoughts are presented, by reading his soliloquies in a sequence. How do his thoughts and his thinking change and in what ways do they stay constant? What are his major preoccupations and his typical manner of self-expression? Now flip this process on its head and focus on Iago's outer life. List all the characters Iago interacts with during the play. For each pairing, write down what the interaction reveals about Iago and about the other character. How does Iago act and speak differently when talking to different characters? Compare, for example, how he talks to Roderigo with how he addresses Cassio.

Thought-tracking: Pick a scene and imagine you can freeze the action at any five points. Once the action is frozen, zoom into any of the characters' thoughts. Either you could focus on one character's thoughts or range more widely. It might also be interesting to speculate on the hidden thoughts of characters who are listening rather than speaking.

Probe, hook, deflect, block. This exercise involves thinking about how characters use words to try to influence each other. Pick a scene or section of a scene featuring only two of three characters, such as one of exchanges between Othello and Iago. For each exchange of the dialogue decide whether the lines ask questions of the other character [probe], try to intrigue and draw them in [hook], avoid answering any questions by switching topic [deflect] or outright refuse to engage [block]. Similarly imagine staging the scene. Work out who would be standing where and how each character will move at various key points. Does Iago stand behind Othello? Does Othello try to walk away from him? Think too of eye contact. When do the characters look at each other, straight in the eyes, and when might they avoid eye contact?

Walking out a soliloquy. You'll need a bit of space for this exercise and ideally more than one person. One person needs to get up and begin reading a soliloquy. As they read, they should walk forward slowly in a straight line until they reach a piece of punctuation. At this point, decide whether to carry on walking in the same direction, to deviate a little, turn ninety degrees in one direction or even turn volte face. The exercise will help you to map out the pattern of Iago and Othello's thoughts and make the abstract more tangible. After completing the exercise, watch a soliloquy in a couple of different productions. What do these performances share with your interpretation and how are they different from each other and from your own mapping?

Who's most to blame? This exercise works best in a classroom setting. The teacher puts names of the principal characters on different tables. When the class enters the room, they have to walk around the tables and then choose to stand next to the one showing the character they think is most to blame. Once everyone has decided, going around the tables each in turn, the pupils should try to persuade other pupils to come to their table.

Repeat the exercise above, but add another possible culprit. The pupils who pick another element as the main cause of the tragedy should each write down who or what they consider this other to be [perhaps Fortinbras or the socio-historical context or uncertainty about the ethics of revenge]. Replace the characters' names with this new set of possible culprits on the tables and repeat the exercise for a final time. Now all the pupils should be ready to tackle an essay based on this question.

Chapter-style titles for scenes, scrambled.

[We have used a mixture of quotations and our own words for chapter titles, and in one case suggested two possible titles]

1. Cassio's Disgrace
2. Safely in Cyprus
3. Work on my medicine work
4. I hope my lord esteems me honest or The Moor's abused by some villainous knave
5. Death of Roderigo
6. Darkness and Duplicity in Venice
7. 'Twas I that killer her.
8. The Herald
9. Let Music be the Food of Love
10. These letters, Iago
11. Keep up your Bright Swords
12. I do not think but Desdemona's honest
13. The Lost Handkerchief and the fair devil
14. The Senate Decides
15. The Willow Song

Total: 15

Analysing an Extract

This sort of task often features on A-Level and GCSE specifications, including currently AQA B at A-level and CAIE at IGCSE. Though AQA tasks examine the selected passage through specific lenses [through the thematic lenses of love or tragedy], the main foci for the examination questions are on the presentation of characters through language and/or what makes a scene dramatically effective. All the questions test the quality of understanding and assess the skill of close reading of language.

We're going to work through one example on *Othello* taken from AQA's A-level specimen assessment material. Though the approach we take has AQA's A-level style of question in mind, it should be easily adaptable to other specifications and to students reading the play at GCSE level.

A quick word of advice on the structure of your essay. We strongly advise that your essay does not work chronologically through the text from opening to final line. Nor should you try to summarise the action. If your essay starts with 'in the first line of the text' or you find yourself using chronological discourse markers, such as 'then', 'after', 'before' and 'when' you'll know you're losing your analytical focus and your examiner will be tutting and muttering darkly to themselves. A paragraph starting 'Then Othello says to Iago that...' is likely to develop into narrative summary. This is always to be avoided as it's worth very few marks.

In contrast, examiners will be delighted by, and handsomely reward, perceptive, assured close reading, well informed by your studies. By perceptive they mean spotting what is not immediately obvious, reading between the lines, picking up subtext, being alert to the nuances of technique and specific choices of language. 'Assured' suggests your reading should be rooted in strong knowledge and understanding of the text and of ways of reading it.

AQA B Specimen Question: Othello – William Shakespeare

Explore the significance of the aspects of dramatic tragedy in the following passage in relation to the play as a whole. [25 marks]

You should consider the following in your answer:
- the presentation of Iago and Othello
- the dramatic setting
- other relevant aspects of dramatic tragedy.

Venice Outside the Saggitary
Enter Othello, Iago, attendants with torches

IAGO
Though in the trade of war I have slain men,
Yet do I hold it very stuff o'th' conscience
To do no contrived murder: I lack iniquity
Sometimes to do me service. Nine or ten times
I had thought t'have yerked him here under the ribs.

OTHELLO
'Tis better as it is.

IAGO
Nay, but he prated
And spoke such scurvy and provoking terms
Against your honour,
That with the little godliness I have,
I did full hard forbear him. But I pray, sir,
Are you fast married? For be assured of this,
That the Magnifico is much beloved,
And hath in his effect a voice potential
As double as the Duke's. He will divorce you,
Or put upon you what restraint and grievance
That law, with all his might to enforce it on,
Will give him cable.

OTHELLO
Let him do his spite:
My services, which I have done the signory,
Shall out-tongue his complaints. 'Tis yet to know –
Which, when I know that boasting is an honour,
I shall provulgate – I fetch my life and being
From men of royal siege, and my demerits
May speak, unbonneted, to as proud a fortune
As this that I have reached. For know, Iago,
But that I love the gentle Desdemona,
I would not my unhousèd free condition
Put into circumscription and confine
For the seas' worth. But look, what lights come yond!

IAGO
Those are the raisèd father and his friends:
You were best go in.

OTHELLO Not I: I must be found.
My parts, my title, and my perfect soul
Shall manifest me rightly. Is it they?

IAGO
By Janus, I think no.
Enter Cassio, with men bearing torches

OTHELLO
The servants of the Duke and my Lieutenant!
The goodness of the night upon you, friends.
What is the news?

CASSIO
The Duke does greet you, General,
And he requires your haste-post-haste appearance
Even on the instant.

OTHELLO
What is the matter, think you?

CASSIO
Something from Cyprus, as I may divine:
It is a business of some heat. The galleys
Have sent a dozen sequent messengers
This very night at one another's heels;
And many of the consuls, raised and met,
Are at the Duke's already. You have been hotly called for,
When being not at your lodging to be found.
The senate hath sent about three several quests
To search you out.

OTHELLO
'Tis well I am found by you:
I will but spend a word here in the house
And go with you.

Exit
[Act I, Scene 2]

It's possible that over time AQA will advise candidates to answer each of the three bullet points in sequence, perhaps even separately. We're going to assume that the response required is a coherent essay which treats the bullet points as prompts for discussion. We should point out that what follows isn't in itself meant to be an exemplar answer. See it rather as a guide to the sort of analysis the boards are after.

Where should we start? It's always helpful to begin with an overview. Establish the big picture first. In your introduction outline the aspects which you're going to go on to examine more closely in the main body of the essay. In this instance, we'd start with contexts. The scene is from Act I, Sc. 2 so it comes very early in the play; indeed, it is the first time Othello appears on stage.

Crucially, however, he has already been described by Iago and Roderigo in the previous scene, so expectations about his character have already been established and could now be confirmed. Or confounded. The play's narrative structure is also significant: we also already know that Iago secretly hates Othello and is plotting against him. Hence this scene is full of dramatic irony; we, the audience, know Iago is duplicitous; Othello and the other characters do not.

Shakespeare must strike a delicate dramatic balance in his use of dramatic irony: Iago must perform the role of dutiful, loyal servant convincingly enough for the other characters to believe in it. However, Shakespeare also needs to signal to the audience what Iago is really up to – trying to sow seeds of contention between Othello and other characters and in the process undermine his master's authority, without this being blindingly obvious. If this signalling is too overt, Othello will be made to look a fool and the audience will lose sympathy for the tragic hero.

We've also to consider this scene through the lens of tragedy. So, we should comment on the fact that the scene features the tragic hero and hints at a number of potential causes of his downfall. For instance, external forces, such  as a villainous enemy, Othello's outsider status in Venice as a Moor in a Christian culture and the wider context of conflict between Venice and Turkey, as introduced by Cassio. Aristotle's term 'hamartia' refers to a flaw in the protagonist or the protagonist's behaviour. Potential internal sources of tragedy could include Othello's difficulty in perceiving Iago's double dealing, arguably his arrogance or even hubris [psychological flaws] as well as the potentially poor decisions he makes, specifically secretly marrying Desdemona, promoting Cassio over Iago, trusting Iago and never listening to his wife's protestations of innocence.

On to the setting. Here the setting is a street in the city state of Venice outside an inn, crucially, in darkness. Each of these three details is significant. We're sure you'll be able to say something about the importance of Venice, particularly for a Renaissance audience. Limit your consideration of Venice to one or two sentences and make it relevant to this passage, as contextual information simply regurgitated from notes would set an examiner frowning. Broadly, as discussed earlier in this guide, for Shakespeare's contemporaries Venice denotes a cultured, orderly and civilised society, potentially under threat from what they considered to be non-Christian barbarians. The fact that Othello is the 'Moor of Venice' resonates with this socio-political context. The fact that he is found outside an inn, in the streets is also significant. Inns in Shakespeare's plays are often associated with low life characters and rough, sordid action. This is not the natural or fitting location for noble characters or noble behaviour. Thus, it adds to the sense of unease. Darkness obviously further enhances this, literally making characters and the audience uncertain about what is happening, but also symbolically suggesting immorality, dark deeds, ignorance and so forth.

How does the setting link to the characters? Certainly, it suits Iago's Machiavellian character and dark machinations. What else do we learn about him in this scene? Firstly, that he's a great actor; he can perform different roles dextrously. Iago requires Othello to believe he is a straightforward, plain-speaking, reliable and loyal soldierly servant. So, this is how he presents himself. Hence his speech about being provoked to violently defend Othello's honour and his soldierly ethical distinctions about killings in battle and in civilian life. Underneath the mask of solid reliability and loyal concern, however, Iago quickly stokes unease, insinuating that Othello's marriage may be the cause of violent discord between the Moor and the most powerful figures in Venice.

Iago's first attempts to unsettle Othello fail. So he has to up the rhetorical ante. Employing emotive and inflammatory language, he utilises imagery of disease: 'such scurvy and provoking terms'. Notice how unspecific Iago is about the details. He does not tell us what had actually been said or by whom or why he was almost driven to murder. Presenting themselves as transparently informative, Iago's words are actually hooks, baited to snag Othello and tug at his self-assurance. The pun on 'fast' to mean hasty, but also secure, for instance, attempts to shake Othello's confidence in his marriage, a tactic Iago will develop further as the play goes on. Iago also introduces legal language to imply that Othello might be arrested for his actions, 'restraint', 'law', 'grievance' and 'enforce'. His reaction to the appearance of the torches ['You had best go in')] is typical of how he pretends to be acting to protect Othello's best interests, but actually seeks to alarm Othello and to stir up all the trouble he can. Hence his claim that the torches are being carried by Brabantio and his followers.

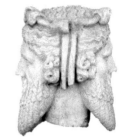

Why does Iago swear 'by Janus', a double-headed God who simultaneously looks in opposite directions? Perhaps Shakespeare gives him this line to ensure the theatre audience has properly understood Iago's double-dealing nature. Possibly an inattentive audience could have been taken in by Iago's impressive impersonation of honest servant. Plays are written to be performed, obviously, and different directors and actors will interpret characters differently. Iago could, for instance, be played as a rather nervous character, on edge in case his villainy is discovered. Or he could be played as a confident, smiling Machiavel, a villain who takes sadistic pleasure from hoodwinking his master with consummate ease. In this second interpretation, 'by Janus' could be performed as a sort of metaphorical nudge and wink to the audience, a 'look at me, see what I'm doing?' – Iago enjoying vaunting his true diabolical nature right under Othello's nose.

This leads us to consider how we react to Iago at this point in the play. Later, of course, we will be taken into his plans and made queasily complicit in them through Shakespeare's use of soliloquies. But even here, different readers and audiences will respond differently, in part depending on how the characters are played. We might, for instance, be impressed by Iago's skill and cleverness, or we may already be repulsed by his betrayal of his noble master. Our reaction to Iago depends largely on how we respond to Othello.

As we have already mentioned, Othello has already been described in scene 1 through the poisonous, racist language used by Iago and Roderigo. How he appears in this scene utterly belies this description. Othello's first words in the play, for instance, are simple and direct, contrasting in their calmness with Iago's urgent agitated tone. The tragic hero's composure and control of the situation is evinced by the way he interrupts Iago's line, halting the hurried onward flow of words with five powerfully dismissive monosyllables: 'Let him do his spite'. That composure is further underlined by the incomplete line, an embedded stage direction that implies a pause after the word 'spite'. Later when the torches are seen and Iago tries to unnerve Othello by implying there might be violent trouble – 'you were best go in' – Othello is again unflustered, and again using similarly simple, direct language to emphasise his calm command of himself and the situation: 'Not I, I must be found'.

Generally, of course, Othello's style of speech is declarative, measured and, at times, rather grand. He comes across as a character used to being listened to. We learn that his self-assurance rests on his royal heritage and the brave deeds he has done. There is, however, some indication of a chink in his armour; his admission that he is not totally familiar yet with Venetian cultural etiquette [he has not broadcast his heritage as yet because he is unsure about whether this boasting would be deemed dishonourable]. Later in the play Iago will, of course, use Othello's outsider status against him. Another potential Achilles heel is his marriage to Desdemona, which Othello admits may in some ways 'confine' him and make him vulnerable to control - 'circumscription'. This acknowledgement of potential weakness is music to Iago's ears and ammunition for his scheming.

Othello's elevated idiom and elegant syntax may be distinct from Iago's plainer language in this scene, but they share a soldierly mentality. We see this in Othello's claim that his actions will speak for him: 'my services...shall out-tongue'. This impression is reinforced by his reference to 'unbonneted', a metaphor that suggests he values language that is plain, not dressed up or disguised in any way. It is part of a group of phrases in this passage that highlight the importance of language: 'He prated'; 'provoking terms'; 'a voice'; 'out-tongue'. As we shall see, Othello's noble actions will be fatally undermined by Iago's brilliant use of words as masks and weapons.

Perhaps then, there is a degree of naivety to Othello that could be read as his hamartia. In particular, he is naïve in trusting Iago and about how he is viewed in Venice. He also trusts Iago's words because they are expressed seemingly plainly. Isn't there also something arrogant too about his unruffled self-assurance? His reference to his 'perfect soul' seems, in particular, hubristic.

Overall, in this short extract Othello is presented as a tower of strength, a tower that Venetian society depends on when threatened by external enemies. The foundations of Othello's strength rest on his noble relationships with other characters, including his wife. As the play develops, he will lean ever more heavily on one of these characters, his faithful seeming servant 'honest' Iago. We know that Iago is in fact constantly chipping away at those foundations in order that, eventually, the tower will topple, and seemingly of its own accord. This set-up is what makes this scene and many others in the play dramatically compelling.

As the critic Anthony Brennan has written, the peculiar dramatic intensity and dramatic success of this tragedy 'depends on arousing our impulsive wish to stop the action' to warn Othello and the other characters of the danger they are in, 'and that the more, as civilised playgoers, we stifle that impulse the more the play achieves its ascendancy over us'. It is not simply that we lack the release valve provided in pantomime but rather that we are confronted again and again by our helplessness'.[7] That dynamic is established in Act I and continues to hold us in its grip until the curtain falls four Acts later.

---

[7] Anthony Brennan, Iago, *The Strategist of Separation*.

GLOSSARY

ALIENATION EFFECT – coined by German playwright, Berthold Brecht, it reverses the conventional idea that audiences suspend their disbelief when watching a play

ANTITHESIS – the use of balanced opposites, at sentence or text level

APOSTROPHE – a figure of speech addressing a person, object or idea

ASIDE – words spoken for only the audience to hear

CADENCE – the rise and fall of sounds in a line

CATHARSIS – a feeling of release an audience supposedly feels at the end of a tragedy

CONCEIT – an extended metaphor

DRAMATIC IRONY – when the audience knows things the on-stage characters do not

FIGURATIVE LANGUAGE – language that is not literal, but employs figures of speech, such as metaphor, simile and personification

FOURTH WALL – the term for the invisible wall separating the audience and the actors on the stage

GOTHIC – a style of literature characterised by psychological horror, dark deeds and uncanny events

HAMARTIA – a tragic or fatal flaw in the protagonist of a tragedy that contributes significantly to their downfall

HEROIC COUPLETS – pairs of rhymed lines in iambic pentameter

HYPERBOLE – extreme exaggeration

IAMBIC – a metrical pattern of a weak followed by a strong stress, ti-TUM, like a heart beat

IMAGERY – the umbrella term for description in poetry. Sensory imagery refers to descriptions that appeal to sight, sound and so forth; figurative imagery refers to the use of devices such as metaphor, simile and personification

JUXTAPOSITION – two things placed together to create a strong contrast

METAPHOR – an implicit comparison in which one thing is said to be another

METONYM – when something closely associated with a thing stands in for that thing, such as a book representing education

METRE – the regular pattern organising sound and rhythm in a poem

MONOLOGUE – extended speech by a single character

MOTIF – a repeated image or pattern of language, often carrying thematic significance

ONOMATOPOEIA – bang, crash, wallop

PENTAMETER – a poetic line consisting of fives stressed beats

PERSONIFICATION – giving human characteristics to inanimate things

PLOSIVE – a type of alliteration using 'p' and 'b' sounds

ROMANTIC – a type of poetry characterised by a love of nature, by strong emotion and heightened tone

SIMILE – an explicit comparison of two different things

SOLILOQUY – a speech by a single character alone on stage revealing their innermost thoughts

STAGECRAFT – a term for all the stage devices used by a playwright, encompassing lighting, costume, music, directions and so forth

STICHOMYTHIA – quick, choppy exchanges of dialogue between characters

SUSPENSION OF DISBELIEF – the idea that the audience willingly treats the events on stage as if they were real

SYMBOL – something that stands in for something else. Often a concrete representation of an idea.

SYNECDOCHE – when the part of something represents the whole, such as the crown for the British monarchy.

SYNTAX – the word order in a sentence. Syntax is crucial to sense: For example, though it uses all the same words, 'the man eats the fish' is not the same as 'the fish eats the man'

TRAGEDY – a play that ends with the deaths of the main characters

UNITIES – A description of a play's tragic structure by Aristotle that relates to three elements of time, place and action

WELL-MADE PLAY – a type of play that follows specific conventions so that its action looks and feels realistic.

Chapter-style titles for scenes; correct order

1. Darkness and Duplicity in Venice
2. Keep up your Bright Swords
3. The Senate Decides
4. Safely in Cyprus
5. The Herald
6. Cassio's Disgrace
7. Let Music be the Food of Love
8. These letters, Iago
9. I do not think but Desdemona's honest
10. The Lost Handkerchief and the fair devil
11. Work on my medicine work
12. I hope my lord esteems me honest or The Moor's abused by some villainous knave
13. The Willow Song
14. Death of Roderigo
15. 'Twas I that killer her.

Recommended Reading

Gibson, R. *Othello*. CUP, 2002.

Maguire, L. *Studying Shakespeare.* Wiley & Sons, 2013.

McEachern, C. *The Cambridge Companion to Shakespearian Tragedy.* CUP, 2013.

McEvoy, S. *Shakespeare the Basics.* Routledge, 2006.

Palfrey, S. *Doing Shakespeare.* Arden, 2005.

Ryan, K. Shakespearean Tragedy, Bloomsbury, 2021.

Smith, E. *This is Shakespeare.* Pelican, 2019.

Websites

The British Library, *Discovering Shakespeare*

The English & Media Centre have many great articles on *Othello*

Massolit

Peripeteia.webs.com

Useful theorists & critics

Theorists of Tragedy
Aristotle
Hegel
Nietzsche

Traditional Criticism
A.C. Bradley
Samuel Taylor Coleridge
Helen Gardner
G. Wilson Knight
F.R. Leavis

Modern Criticism
Jonathan Dollimore
Marilyn French
Stephen Greenblatt
Andrew Hadfield
Lisa Hopkins
Lisa Jardine
Ania Loomba
Sean McEvoy
Kiernan Ryan
Emma Smith

About the authors

Head of English and writer, Neil Bowen has a Master's Degree in Literature & Education from the University of Cambridge and is a member of Ofqual's experts panel for English. He is the author of *The Art of Writing English Essays for GCSE*, co-author and editor of *The Art of Writing English Essays for A-level*, *The Art of Poetry*, *The Art of Literature* and *The Art of Drama* series. Neil runs the peripeteia project, bridging the gap between A-level and degree level English courses **www.peripeteia.webs.com**, regularly delivers talks at GCSE & A-level student conferences and occasionally CPD sessions for fellow teachers.

A PhD student at Royal Holloway University, researching women's work in the nineteenth-century novel, Johanna Harrison-Oram holds degrees in English from the University of Oxford and from KCL and in Music from the Guildhall School of Music and Drama. The Deputy Editor of the Romance, Revolution & Reform journal at the University of Southampton, she has contributed to several books in the *Art of Poetry* series.

Alice Penfold works for Woodard Academies Trust as an English Curriculum Lead. She is a former Pedagogy Lead and English teacher, most recently working as Assistant Subject Lead for English and whole-school Reading Lead. Currently studying for a PhD, focused on language, gender and identity in young adult fantasy fiction, Alice has written educational resources and presented at numerous conferences, including ResearchEd, the National Association of Writers in Education (NAWE) and the Open University UK Literacy Association (UKLA).

An Irish English teacher, Michael Meally holds an MA in American Literature as well as first class degrees in English Literature and Engineering. Michael is the co-author of *The Art of Writing English Literature Essays* and has contributed to many of the *Art of Poetry* and *Art of Drama* books.

Ingram Content Group UK Ltd.
Milton Keynes UK
UKHW021936040723
424555UK00008B/795